"Let's win one for the Gipper."
—Knute Rockne

101 REASONS TO LOVE NOTRE DAME FOOTBALL

DAVID GREEN

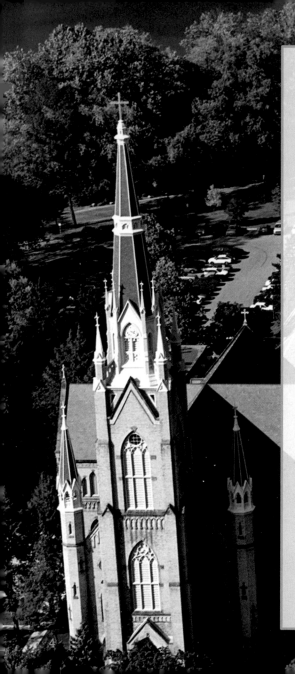

INTRODUCTION

I grew up in North Carolina watching Atlantic Coast Conference teams such as UNC, Duke, and Wake Forest play football back in the 1960s and '70s. My father was a sportswriter, and I was lucky enough to attend many games with him. I found the atmosphere surrounding the games to be mesmerizing—a mixture of invigorating energy and romantic drama—the stuff dreams, and books, are made of.

Walking across those beautiful campuses—painted in fall colors, the crowd abuzz with anticipation and the collective energy of hope, honor, devotion, and spirit—was something out of a Norman Rockwell painting.

But as big and grand as all that seemed to me, I could still go home and turn on the television and watch a college team that transcended all the rest.

Notre Dame football. Nothing matched it then, and as much as other programs want to boast these days, nothing really matches the history and tradition at Notre Dame now. Sure, those other programs have had their days in the sun, their names inscribed on championship trophies or atop the final polls, but none has accomplished what Notre Dame has.

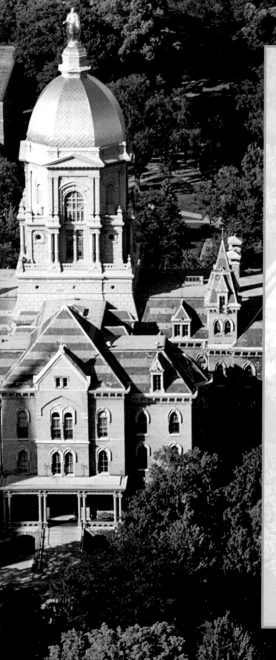

Notre Dame is at the top of the list in national championships, Heisman Trophy winners, and all-time winning percentage. But more than that, the legacy of the university itself, and all the people it has so profoundly influenced—students, parents, teachers, and everyday citizens—is beyond compare.

Governors and members of Congress have been educated there. So have Supreme Court justices and business leaders. Generals and astronauts. Nobel Prize winners and award-winning authors. And those ordinary folks who go out and give their all, do their best, and try to make the world a better place.

That's what they learn at Notre Dame. On the football field and off. This book is a celebration of that, so…

Rally sons of Notre Dame:
Sing her glory and sound her fame,
Raise her Gold and Blue
And cheer with voices true:
Rah, rah, for Notre Dame

1 THE UNIVERSITY OF NOTRE DAME

Few universities in the land boast the heritage and accomplishments of this great institution, located in South Bend, Indiana. Founded in 1842 by 28-year-old French priest Father Edward Sorin, of the Congregation of Holy Cross, the university originally consisted of three decrepit log buildings and Father Sorin's dreams. Today, it is one of the premier educational institutions in America.

Nestled just south of the Michigan-Indiana state line, Notre Dame's campus is one of the most breathtakingly beautiful in the United States. The changing leaves of hardwoods render the campus in reds, golds, and yellows, creating the iconic imagery associated with college football, and the snows of winter, courtesy of nearby Lake Michigan, bring forth a frozen wonderland that's truly a work of art. Coupled with the enduring majesty of the historical Main Building with its golden dome, and the Basilica of the Sacred Heart, the campus of Notre Dame is an inspiration to all who visit—students, faculty, artists, and athletes—and especially those who choose to stay.

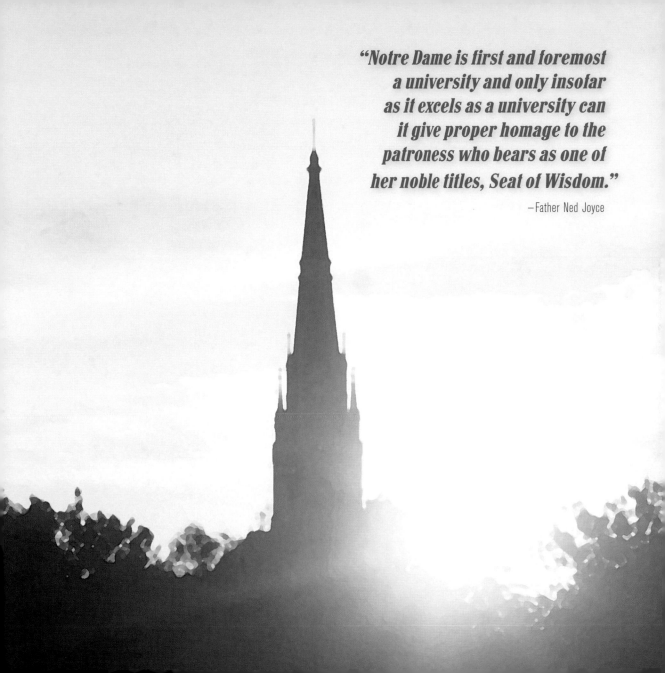

"Notre Dame is first and foremost a university and only insofar as it excels as a university can it give proper homage to the patroness who bears as one of her noble titles, Seat of Wisdom."

—Father Ned Joyce

2 WHEN IT ALL BEGAN

Way back in 1887, a group of student athletes at Notre Dame decided to form a football club. A team from the University of Michigan, which had been playing the game for 10 years, came to South Bend to offer instruction and then faced the Notre Dame squad in its first official game. Despite the large gap in experience, the white flannel–clad "Catholics" held their own, losing 8–0. The first win for the Catholics came the following year when they defeated Harvard School of Chicago, 20–0.

3 THE FIGHTING IRISH

It's not entirely clear where the nickname came from, but the widely accepted story is that the phrase was generally used as a derogatory expression in the beginning. It was picked up and popularized by the press, and "Fighting Irish" came to represent teams with true grit, mettle, and determination. Also known for a time as the Catholics and the Ramblers, Notre Dame officially adopted the Fighting Irish moniker in 1927, and it has become one of the most universally recognized nicknames in all of sports.

> *"The unkind appellation became symbolic of the struggle for supremacy on the field."*
>
> – The Notre Dame Scholastic, 1929

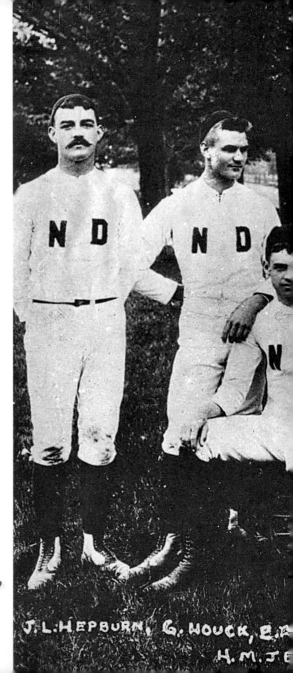

J.L. HEPBURN, G. HOUCK, E.A
H.M.J.E

AWKINS. F. FEHR, P. NELSON G. MELADY, F. SPRINGER.
ETT, J.E. CUSACK H.B.LUHN. E. PRUDHOOME.

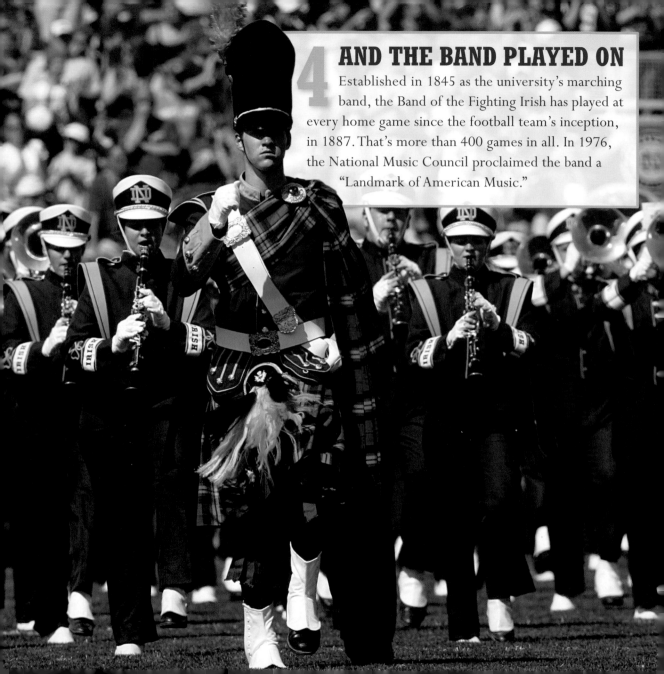

4 AND THE BAND PLAYED ON

Established in 1845 as the university's marching band, the Band of the Fighting Irish has played at every home game since the football team's inception, in 1887. That's more than 400 games in all. In 1976, the National Music Council proclaimed the band a "Landmark of American Music."

5 THE VICTORY MARCH

Notre Dame's fight song, the "Notre Dame Victory March," was written by alumni and brothers Michael and John Shea in the early 1900s and copyrighted in 1908. One of the most recognizable fight songs in all of sports, it was first performed at a Notre Dame athletic event in 1919 and has since become a piece of American culture, honored as the "greatest of all fight songs" at the centennial celebration of college football in 1969.

Rally sons of Notre Dame:
Sing her glory and sound her fame,
Raise her Gold and Blue
And cheer with voices true:
Rah, rah, for Notre Dame
We will fight in ev-ry game,
Strong of heart and true to her name
We will ne'er forget her
And will cheer her ever
Loyal to Notre Dame

Cheer, cheer for old Notre Dame,
Wake up the echoes cheering her name,
Send a volley cheer on high,
Shake down the thunder from the sky.
What though the odds be great or small
Old Notre Dame will win over all,
While her loyal sons are marching
Onward to victory.

Left: The marching band of Notre Dame
Inset: 1890 band

6 291–0

That's the cumulative score for the 1903 season, when Notre Dame went 8–0–1. The only blemish on its record was a 0–0 tie versus Northwestern.

7 RED SALMON

Fullback Louis "Red" Salmon captained the 1903 squad, which went undefeated with one tie. Considered the first great Irish back, Salmon tallied 250 points in his career, including 105 as a senior, at a time when touchdowns counted for only five points. His record wasn't broken for 82 years, when Allen Pinkett scored 320 points from 1982 to 1985.

8 142–0

Yes, you read that correctly. On October 28, 1905, Notre Dame demolished American Medical College, 142–0, setting a record for most points ever scored in a game. With the score 111–0 at halftime, the teams elected to play an eight-minute second half. Notre Dame still managed to score 31 more points. The Irish recorded 27 touchdowns—27!—and could have tallied an even higher point total had they not missed 20 of 27 extra-point attempts.

"When I was a boy, for me the symbol of Notre Dame was not the Golden Dome. It was a living personality, a redheaded fullback.... It is the Notre Dame that Red Salmon represented, and still represents in my memory, for which I carry an affection transcending an old man's discomfort in the face of change."

—Herb Juliano

Scoring on Michigan '09.

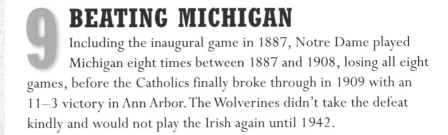

9 BEATING MICHIGAN

Including the inaugural game in 1887, Notre Dame played Michigan eight times between 1887 and 1908, losing all eight games, before the Catholics finally broke through in 1909 with an 11–3 victory in Ann Arbor. The Wolverines didn't take the defeat kindly and would not play the Irish again until 1942.

10 MANY HAPPY RETURNS

Joe Savoldi (1930), Clint Johnson (1993), and Julius Jones (2000) hold the record for the longest kickoff return for a touchdown by a Notre Dame player, each going 100 yards for the score. But Alfred Bergman holds the team record for the longest return ever. Bergman ran a kickoff back 105 yards in a game versus Loyola of Chicago in 1911—only to be tackled at the Loyola 5-yard line. At the time, the field was 110 yards long, and Bergman was pulled down just short of glory after starting from his own goal line.

11 JESSE HARPER

Following four relatively successful years at Wabash College in Indiana, Harper was hired as the head coach of Notre Dame in 1913. Recognizing the talents of quarterback Gus Dorais and end Knute Rockne, Harper made the rarely used forward pass a major component of the Irish offense and led Notre Dame to a record of 34–5–1 over five seasons, bringing the team national recognition it had not previously enjoyed. Harper later served as athletic director for Notre Dame for a few years following Rockne's death.

12 A PASSING FANCY

In the fall of 1913, after traveling by train to West Point, New York, to face Army with only 18 players and 14 pairs of cleats, Notre Dame served notice that it was a national power to be reckoned with. Surprising the Army defense, and football enthusiasts around the country, with a well-executed aerial assault mixed in with its sturdy ground game, Notre Dame rolled to a 35–13 dismantling of the mighty Cadets, scoring 28 unanswered points after trailing, 13–7, in the second quarter. Quarterback Gus Dorais completed 14 of 17 passes and finished the game with 243 yards passing—a truly staggering total at the time—including a record-setting 40-yard completion to senior end Knute Rockne.

Knute Rockne, right, heads for the end zone after catching a pass from Gus Dorais versus Army, 1913. Inset: Jesse Harper

13 KNUTE ROCKNE

Rockne is recognized as one of the great coaches in college football history and is probably best known for his "Win one for the Gipper" speech. Rockne enrolled at Notre Dame in 1910 at the age of 22, after spending four years working in the Chicago Post Office to earn enough money for school. A three-sport athlete who also was a member of the baseball and track and field teams, Rockne and quarterback Gus Dorais made the Irish a two-headed monster, adding an effective passing game to their already devastating rushing attack.

Following graduation, Rockne accepted an assistant teaching position at Notre Dame and became an assistant coach under Jesse Harper.

Rockne took over for Harper in 1918 and led the Irish to a cumulative record of 105–12–5 over the next 13 years, only once losing more than two games in a season. Rockne's .881 winning percentage is the best in college and pro football history. His teams posted five undefeated seasons and won three consensus national championships. The first came in 1924, when the "Four Horsemen of the Apocalypse" keyed the Irish attack.

Rockne died in a plane crash in Kansas in 1931, while flying to California to assist in production of the film *The Spirit of Notre Dame*. He was only 43. When the College Football Hall of Fame opened in 1951, Rockne was among the 54 members of the inaugural class.

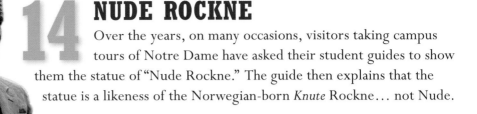

14 NUDE ROCKNE

Over the years, on many occasions, visitors taking campus tours of Notre Dame have asked their student guides to show them the statue of "Nude Rockne." The guide then explains that the statue is a likeness of the Norwegian-born *Knute* Rockne... not Nude.

15 HUNK ANDERSON

Heartley "Hunk" Anderson was a four-year starter from 1918 to 1921, playing under the tutelage of the immortal Knute Rockne. He was a key member of the offensive line that blocked for the great George Gipp, and his teams won 20 consecutive games between 1919 and 1921. As a senior, Anderson blocked two punts and recovered both for touchdowns in a game against Purdue. It was the first time in history a guard had scored twice in a game. He went on to win first-team All-American honors that year. After four years playing pro ball with the Chicago Bears, Anderson returned to South Bend to join Rockne's coaching staff. He took over the head coaching job in 1931 after Rockne's death, and his teams were 16–9–2 in three seasons. Anderson was inducted into the College Football Hall of Fame in 1974.

"Football is not and should not be a game for the strong and stupid. It should be a game for the smart, the swift, the brave, and the clever boy."

–Knute Rockne

16 CURLY LAMBEAU

Earl "Curly" Lambeau became a legend in the National Football League, cofounding the semipro Green Bay Packers in 1919. The team went on to become a charter member of the NFL in 1922, and Lambeau's Packers became the first NFL dynasty, winning six championships between 1929 and 1944. But before that, Lambeau played fullback as a freshman at Notre Dame under rookie coach Knute Rockne. Lambeau was the only freshman to letter that year. He left school his sophomore year after a bout with tonsillitis, going to work in the Indian Packing Company in Green Bay, and the rest is history.

"I felt the thrill that comes to every coach when he knows it is his fate and his responsibility to handle unusual greatness."

–Knute Rockne on George Gipp

George Gipp, with ball, circa 1918

17 GEORGE GIPP

Gipp was practicing drop kicks one day when Coach Knute Rockne spotted him as he strolled across campus. "The Gipper" played for the Notre Dame baseball team but had never played organized football. Despite that, Rockne liked Gipp's athleticism and turned him into one of the best and most versatile players ever to line up for the Irish. Gipp played on both sides of the ball, excelling at halfback and quarterback, and also served as kicker and punter. He led the team in rushing and passing each year from 1918 to 1920, and his career total of 2,341 rushing yards stood as a team record for more than 50 years. Gipp's 1920 average of 86.7 yards rushing per game was extraordinary for the time. He was the first Notre Dame player to be named as a first-team Walter Camp All-American, winning the outstanding player of the year award. Gipp missed the last game of the 1920 season after contracting strep throat and died a few weeks later from pneumonia. He was inducted into the first class of the College Football Hall of Fame in 1951.

1928 Notre Dame–Army game, Yankee Stadium
Inset: Ronald Reagan as George Gipp

18 WIN ONE FOR THE GIPPER

Eight years after the untimely death of George Gipp, Knute Rockne invoked Gipp's memory at halftime of the Notre Dame–Army game in Yankee Stadium. Rallying his troops, Rockne recounted Gipp's deathbed conversation, and the team then went out and defeated Army, 12–6, in front of 85,000 fans.

"I've got to go, Rock. It's all right. I'm not afraid. Some time, Rock, when the team is up against it, when things are wrong and the breaks are beating the boys, ask them to go in there with all they've got and win just one for the Gipper. I don't know where I'll be then, Rock. But I'll know about it, and I'll be happy."

The scene was immortalized in the movie *Knute Rockne, All American*, starring Pat O'Brien as Rockne and Ronald Reagan as Gipp. Reagan later used the slogan in his political campaigns.

19 JOHNNY "ONE PLAY" O'BRIEN

In the legendary "Win One for the Gipper" game versus Army in 1928, the Fighting Irish rallied from a 6–0 second-half deficit to tie the score on a touchdown by running back Jack Chevigny. With the clock winding down, Notre Dame was again driving when a bad snap from the center led to a loss of 16 yards. Faced with a desperate situation, Coach Knute Rockne called on reserve end Johnny O'Brien, who had huddled under a blanket on the bench for more than three quarters. Left halfback Butch Niemiec took the snap from the Army 32, and O'Brien sped down the field, looked over his shoulder to see the ball spiraling his way, reached up, made the catch, and tumbled into the end zone to put the Irish up, 12–6. When Notre Dame stopped Army at the Irish 1 as time expired, it had pinned a historic loss on the previously undefeated West Pointers, and O'Brien's "one play" had become another unforgettable moment in Notre Dame football lore.

20 THE FOUR HORSEMEN

"Outlined against a blue, gray October sky, the Four Horsemen rode again. In dramatic lore they are known as famine, pestilence, destruction and death. These are only aliases. Their real names are: Stuhldreher, Miller, Crowley and Layden."

Don Miller, Elmer Layden, Jim Crowley, and Harry Stuhldreher

Grantland Rice penned this legendary passage for the *New York Herald Tribune* following Notre Dame's 13–7 victory over Army in Yankee Stadium on October 18, 1924. Rockne's student publicity aide, George Strickler, adopted the phrase and arranged the now-iconic photo of the four players clad in their helmets and uniforms astride horses after the team returned to South Bend.

The Irish finished the regular season 9–0 and beat Stanford, 27–10, in the Rose Bowl to win the university's first consensus national football championship.

Harry Stuhldreher: Stuhldreher was the Four Horsemen's quarterback. He was a three-time All-American and, at 5 feet 7 inches tall and 151 pounds, one of the smallest quarterbacks in the history of Notre Dame football.

Don Miller: Right halfback Don Miller was considered by Knute Rockne to be the best open-field runner he ever coached. Miller led the team in rushing in 1923 and 1924, and he posted an average of 6.8 yards per carry for his career. Miller was an All-American selection in 1923.

Jim Crowley: Crowley, the Four Horsemen's left halfback, led the team in scoring in his senior season of 1924 and also earned All-American honors. "Sleepy Jim" often left defenders grasping air with his quick cuts and nimble maneuvers. Crowley went on to coach at Michigan State and Fordham, where Frank Leahy was his defensive line coach.

Elmer Layden: Fullback Elmer Layden anchored the Four Horsemen backfield and won All-American honors in his senior year. The fastest of the four backs, Layden scored three touchdowns in the 1925 Rose Bowl victory over Stanford, including two interception returns that went for scores. Layden later returned to Notre Dame as football coach and athletic director from 1934 to 1940 before leaving to become commissioner of the National Football League in 1941. In his seven seasons as head coach at Notre Dame, his teams went 47–13–3. Although he failed to bring another national championship to South Bend, his 1938 squad finished third in the polls with an 8–1 record.

The Irish won 37 of 41 games while the Four Horsemen were teammates. All four were inducted into the College Football Hall of Fame in 1951.

21 THE SEVEN MULES

Often forgotten in the recounting of the Four Horsemen's exploits is the offensive line that helped open holes for the quartet. These somewhat anonymous laborers were known affectionately as "the Seven Mules." Center Adam Walsh anchored the line and was captain of the 1924 national champions. He went on to coach the Cleveland/Los Angeles Rams in the NFL in 1945 and 1946, winning the championship with Cleveland in 1945. Walsh was inducted into the College Football Hall of Fame in 1968.

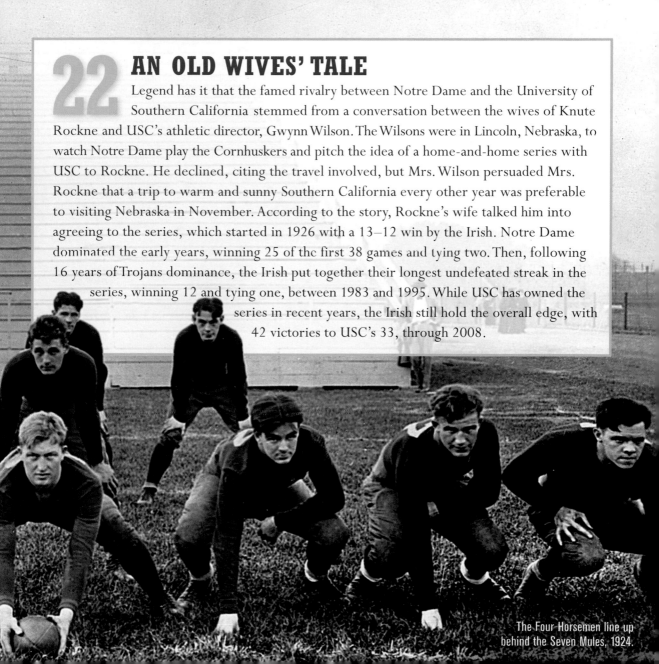

22 AN OLD WIVES' TALE

Legend has it that the famed rivalry between Notre Dame and the University of Southern California stemmed from a conversation between the wives of Knute Rockne and USC's athletic director, Gwynn Wilson. The Wilsons were in Lincoln, Nebraska, to watch Notre Dame play the Cornhuskers and pitch the idea of a home-and-home series with USC to Rockne. He declined, citing the travel involved, but Mrs. Wilson persuaded Mrs. Rockne that a trip to warm and sunny Southern California every other year was preferable to visiting Nebraska in November. According to the story, Rockne's wife talked him into agreeing to the series, which started in 1926 with a 13–12 win by the Irish. Notre Dame dominated the early years, winning 25 of the first 38 games and tying two. Then, following 16 years of Trojans dominance, the Irish put together their longest undefeated streak in the series, winning 12 and tying one, between 1983 and 1995. While USC has owned the series in recent years, the Irish still hold the overall edge, with 42 victories to USC's 33, through 2008.

The Four Horsemen line up behind the Seven Mules, 1924.

23 ON THE ROAD AGAIN

Knute Rockne was suffering from acute phlebitis in 1929, which confined him to either a bed or a wheelchair much of the time. To make matters even more difficult, the Fighting Irish played all of their games away from home while Notre Dame Stadium was under construction. Despite all the obstacles, Rockne led the team to a 9–0 record and its second consensus national championship in six years. More than 112,000 spectators crammed into Soldier Field in Chicago to watch Notre Dame edge USC, 13–12—the largest confirmed attendance in the history of NCAA football. In the season finale versus Army, Jack Elder returned an interception 100 yards for the game's only score, giving the Irish a 7–0 victory and an undefeated season.

24 JACK CANNON

Cannon, an aggressive and hard-hitting defensive guard, played for Knute Rockne from 1927 to 1929 and was a member of the 1929 national champions. A free spirit, Cannon preferred to play without a helmet, but that didn't dampen his renegade warrior mentality. His contributions were recognized in 1929 when he was named to the All-American team. Cannon was inducted into the College Football Hall of Fame in 1965.

"Without a doubt, he was the best lineman Notre Dame ever turned out."

—Harry Stuhldreher on Jack Cannon

Notre Dame versus USC, 1931

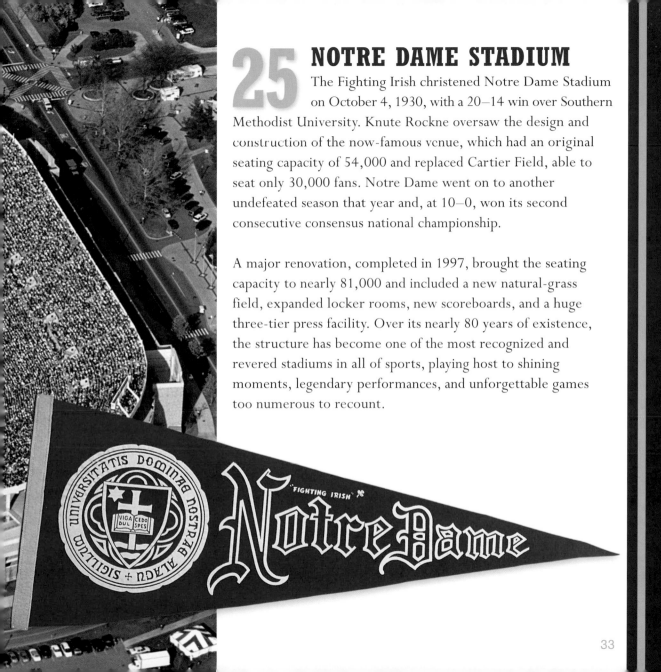

25 NOTRE DAME STADIUM

The Fighting Irish christened Notre Dame Stadium on October 4, 1930, with a 20–14 win over Southern Methodist University. Knute Rockne oversaw the design and construction of the now-famous venue, which had an original seating capacity of 54,000 and replaced Cartier Field, able to seat only 30,000 fans. Notre Dame went on to another undefeated season that year and, at 10–0, won its second consecutive consensus national championship.

A major renovation, completed in 1997, brought the seating capacity to nearly 81,000 and included a new natural-grass field, expanded locker rooms, new scoreboards, and a huge three-tier press facility. Over its nearly 80 years of existence, the structure has become one of the most recognized and revered stadiums in all of sports, playing host to shining moments, legendary performances, and unforgettable games too numerous to recount.

26 THE GAME OF THE CENTURY

The November 2, 1935, matchup in Columbus with top-ranked Ohio State was the first of several Notre Dame contests billed as "the Game of the Century." Both teams were undefeated, and playing before a capacity crowd of more than 81,000, the highly favored Buckeyes rolled to a commanding 13–0 lead over the Fighting Irish at halftime. Former Four Horsemen great Elmer Layden, in his second season as head coach, told his charges, "They won the first half. Now it's your turn. Go out and win this half for yourselves."

Notre Dame held the Buckeyes scoreless in the third quarter but still trailed, 13–0. A Steve Miller touchdown early in the fourth cut the lead to 13–6. Still trailing by a touchdown with three minutes left, Andy Pilney led an 80-yard drive that ended with a 33-yard touchdown pass to Mike Layden, younger brother of Coach Layden. Another missed extra point left the Irish trailing, 13–12, with time running out. Coach Layden called for an onside kick, but the Buckeyes recovered. With Ohio State attempting to run out the clock, Pilney forced the Buckeyes' Dick Beltz to fumble, and the Irish recovered near midfield. On the first play, unable to find any open receivers, Pilney scrambled to the Buckeyes' 19 but had to be carried off the field with an injured knee. Backup Bill Shakespeare came on with half a minute remaining. His first pass was nearly intercepted, but then he found Wayne Miller open in the end zone as the clock ticked down, giving Notre Dame a miraculous 18–13 victory.

27 THE BARD OF STATEN ISLAND

Even if he had never thrown the game-winning touchdown pass in the 1935 "Game of the Century" versus Ohio State, making him an unforgettable, if unlikely, hero, William Shakespeare would be worth mentioning simply because of his name. In addition to his heroics in Columbus, Shakespeare was a major contributor to Notre Dame's success in his junior and senior seasons. An effective runner and passer, Shakespeare excelled at punting, averaging 40 yards per kick, including an 86-yarder versus Pittsburgh in 1935. He won first-team All-American honors that year and was inducted into the College Football Hall of Fame in 1983.

An unidentified Notre Dame player attempts to block an Ohio State punt, 1935.

"*Give me a lead of 14–0 at halftime and I will dictate the final score.*"

—Frank Leahy

28 FRANK LEAHY

After Elmer Layden departed, former Notre Dame lineman Frank Leahy was hired as head coach in 1941. Leahy had been an assistant coach under former Four Horsemen great Jim Crowley at Fordham and had brought Boston College into the national spotlight with 20 wins over two seasons. In his first season at Notre Dame, the relentless taskmaster led the Fighting Irish to an 8–0–1 record, which placed them third in the final AP poll. Controversy followed in 1942 when Leahy introduced the new T-formation, scrapping Knute Rockne's classic box formation. But the move paid off the following year when Notre Dame won the first of four national championships under the man known as "the Master."

After serving two years in the Navy during World War II, Leahy returned to South Bend and led the Irish to three national titles in four years, in 1946, 1947, and 1949, compiling a 36–0–2 record during a period that marked the height of Notre Dame's football dynasty. Leahy was forced to retire after the 1953 season following an attack of acute pancreatitis that had a priest administering last rites to him in the locker room during halftime of a game with Georgia Tech. In 11 seasons at Notre Dame, Leahy's teams finished with a cumulative record of 87–11–9. He was inducted into the College Football Hall of Fame in 1970.

Frank Leahy, kneeling, speaking to his team, 1946

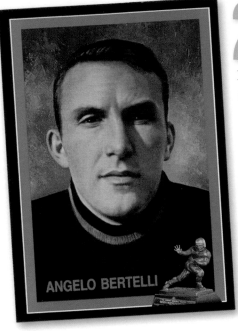

ANGELO BERTELLI

29 THE SPRINGFIELD RIFLE

When Coach Frank Leahy made the switch to the new, modified T-formation, he named Angelo Bertelli his new quarterback. Bertelli had passed for more than 1,000 yards from his tailback position in his sophomore season the year before, making him the first Irish player to eclipse the 1,000-yard mark. Known as "the Springfield Rifle" after his birthplace in West Springfield, Massachusetts, Bertelli threw for 1,039 yards from the T-formation in 1942, with 10 touchdowns, setting a Notre Dame team record. He also intercepted eight passes that year, setting another team record that stood for 20 years. As a senior, Bertelli became the first Notre Dame player to win the Heisman Trophy, passing for more than 500 yards and 10 touchdowns in just six games before he was called into military service. The Irish won their fourth consensus national championship that year, despite losing their finale to Great Lakes a month after Bertelli left for the Marines.

30 CREIGHTON MILLER

Miller, nephew of former Four Horsemen great Don Miller, was an independent-minded halfback under Coach Leahy who refused to participate in spring practices, preferring to play golf instead. His 151 yards rushing versus Northwestern in 1942 set a team record that lasted until 1974. And in 1943, his season total of 911 yards led the nation in rushing, making him the first and only Notre Dame back ever to do so. Miller finished fourth in the Heisman Trophy voting that year, an award won by teammate Angelo Bertelli. Miller was inducted into the College Football Hall of Fame in 1976.

"Bert, you're the finest passer and the worst runner I've ever coached."

—Frank Leahy to Angelo Bertelli

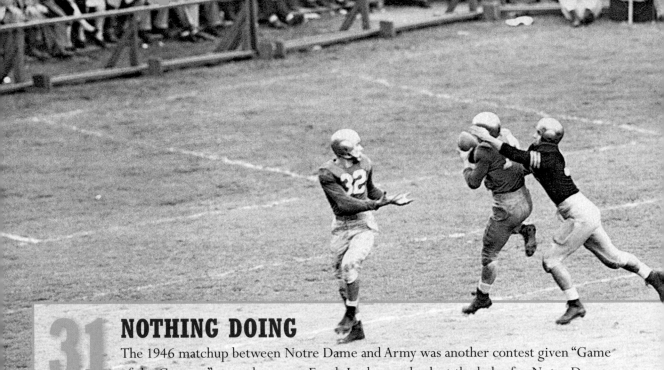

31 NOTHING DOING

The 1946 matchup between Notre Dame and Army was another contest given "Game of the Century" status by many. Frank Leahy was back at the helm for Notre Dame after serving two years in the Navy, and his squad was looking for redemption after the Cadets had pounded the Fighting Irish in the previous two meetings. Both teams came into the game sporting undefeated records, and Army had claimed the national championship in back-to-back seasons in 1944 and 1945. The game, on November 9, was a brutal, defensive struggle yielding few opportunities for scoring. The Irish had a first-and-goal at the Army 4 in the second quarter but came away with nothing when they chose to go for it and failed on fourth down, eschewing a field-goal attempt because Leahy's teams quite simply did not kick field goals. The Fighting Irish defense held Army's great running backs, Doc Blanchard and Glenn Davis, in check, and when Terry Brennan intercepted Davis' option pass at the Irish 8 late in the game, Notre Dame had stopped the Cadets' one real threat and salvaged the scoreless tie. It was the only blemish on Notre Dame's record all season, and the Irish won the national championship with an 8–0–1 record, giving up a total of only 24 points all year.

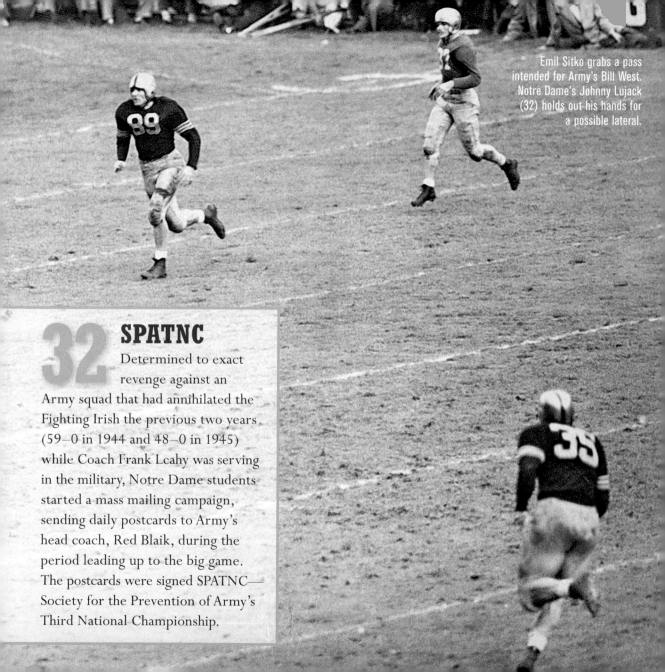

Emil Sitko grabs a pass intended for Army's Bill West. Notre Dame's Johnny Lujack (32) holds out his hands for a possible lateral.

32 SPATNC

Determined to exact revenge against an Army squad that had annihilated the Fighting Irish the previous two years (59–0 in 1944 and 48–0 in 1945) while Coach Frank Leahy was serving in the military, Notre Dame students started a mass mailing campaign, sending daily postcards to Army's head coach, Red Blaik, during the period leading up to the big game. The postcards were signed SPATNC— Society for the Prevention of Army's Third National Championship.

33 JOHNNY LUJACK

Lujack took over the quarterback position for the Fighting Irish when Angelo Bertelli was called into the service during the 1943 season. After serving two years in the military himself, Lujack returned to South Bend and led the team to back-to-back national championships in 1946 and 1947, with a record of 17–0–1 over that span. A four-sport letterman, Lujack won the Heisman Trophy in 1947 and went on to play for the Chicago Bears in the National Football League. He was inducted into the College Football Hall of Fame in 1960.

34 LUJACK'S TACKLE

In the second quarter of the historic 1946 battle between Notre Dame and Army, the Cadets pushed past midfield and into Irish territory for the first and only time all day. The ball went to the Cadets' bruising and powerful back Doc Blanchard, known as "Mr. Inside"—only this time Blanchard scooted outside, around the end, and sped down the sidelines with nothing but the end zone in front of him. Notre Dame's Johnny Lujack was the only man who had any chance at Blanchard. He raced across the field, dove, and caught Blanchard by the ankles, bringing him down at the Notre Dame 37. The tackle saved the game for the Irish, keeping it tied at 0–0, where it would end.

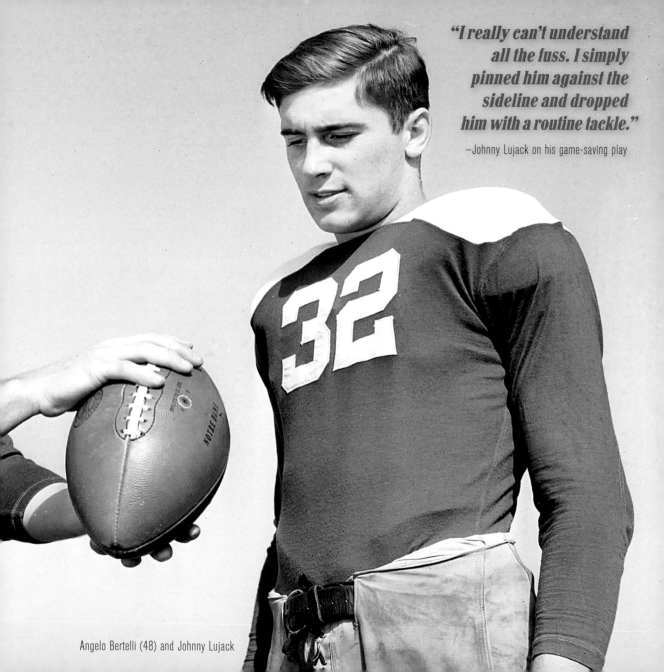

"I really can't understand all the fuss. I simply pinned him against the sideline and dropped him with a routine tackle."

–Johnny Lujack on his game-saving play

Angelo Bertelli (48) and Johnny Lujack

35 1947

Notre Dame won its second consecutive national title in 1947, behind Heisman Trophy winner Johnny Lujack and a dominant offensive line. The Fighting Irish never trailed the entire season, demolishing national powers Army, 27–7, and third-ranked USC, 38–7, on their way to a perfect 9–0 record. In the USC game, Bob Livingstone set a school record with a 92-yard touchdown run, still the longest in Notre Dame history.

36 THE HALL OF FAME LINE

Five members of the offensive line from the 1947 national championship team were inducted into the College Football Hall of Fame: left end Jim Martin, left tackle George Connor, left guard Moose Fischer, right tackle Ziggy Czarobski, and right end Leon Hart.

37 LEON HART

Hart played right end on three Irish national championship squads, including in 1949, when he won the Heisman Trophy. He led the team with 19 receptions for 257 yards, scoring five touchdowns that year. In his four years at Notre Dame, Hart's teams never lost a game, going 36–0–2. The last lineman to win the Heisman, Hart went on to play on three more championship teams, with the Detroit Lions of the NFL. He was inducted into the College Football Hall of Fame in 1973.

Leon Hart hauls in a pass from
Johnny Lujack versus Army, 1947.

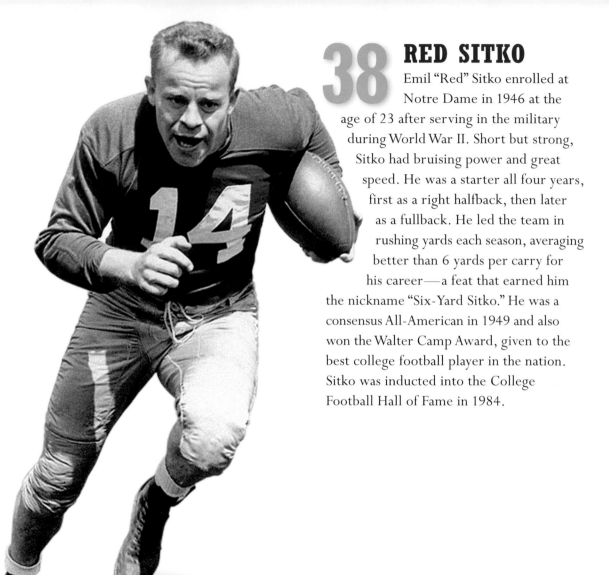

38 RED SITKO

Emil "Red" Sitko enrolled at Notre Dame in 1946 at the age of 23 after serving in the military during World War II. Short but strong, Sitko had bruising power and great speed. He was a starter all four years, first as a right halfback, then later as a fullback. He led the team in rushing yards each season, averaging better than 6 yards per carry for his career—a feat that earned him the nickname "Six-Yard Sitko." He was a consensus All-American in 1949 and also won the Walter Camp Award, given to the best college football player in the nation. Sitko was inducted into the College Football Hall of Fame in 1984.

Right: Notre Dame's John Helwig (49) knocks down a North Carolina pass in the Irish–North Carolina game on November 12, 1949, at Yankee Stadium in New York City.
Left: Emil Sitko

39

1949

When the first polls came out in 1949, Michigan was ranked number one, with Notre Dame second. Following Army's defeat of Michigan in Ann Arbor in early October, the Fighting Irish ascended to the top spot in the polls and remained there for the rest of the year, winning their third national championship in four years under Coach Frank Leahy. Along the way, Notre Dame trounced fourth-ranked Tulane, 46–7, in South Bend, smashed Navy, 40–0, in Baltimore, shut out USC, 32–0, in South Bend, and closed out a perfect season with a tense 27–20 win over Southern Methodist in Dallas when Jerry Groom intercepted Kyle Rote's fourth-down pass from the Irish 5 in the game's waning moments. The win extended the team's undefeated streak to 38 games.

"*It was everybody's game, the whole team made it possible.*"

—Johnny Lattner on the 1952 Notre Dame–Oklahoma game

40 JOHNNY LATTNER

Lattner was a strong, all-purpose back who excelled in every aspect of the game, from 1951 to 1953. For his career, Lattner ran for 1,724 yards, averaging nearly 5 yards per carry and scoring 20 touchdowns. His 3,095 all-purpose yards was an Irish record until 1979, when Vagas Ferguson broke it. He also intercepted 13 passes. Lattner won the Heisman Trophy in 1953, in one of the closest votes ever, edging Paul Giel from Minnesota. He also won the Maxwell Award as the nation's top player in both 1952 and 1953. Lattner was inducted into the College Football Hall of Fame in 1979.

41 IRISH BOOKENDS

The first-ever meeting between Notre Dame and Oklahoma, on November 8, 1952, was a memorable—and nationally televised—game setting in motion a sequence of events that would come full circle five years later. Bud Wilkinson's Oklahoma team came into South Bend heavily favored, sporting a high-powered offense that was averaging 42 points a game and a 13-game unbeaten streak. Despite a bevy of turnovers by both teams in the first half, the Sooners took a 14–7 edge into the locker room behind two Billy Vessels touchdowns. The teams exchanged touchdowns in the third quarter, and when Tom Carey scored from the 1 early in the fourth, the Irish led 27–21. Notre Dame's defense then stopped three consecutive Sooner drives that reached deep into Irish territory, and Notre Dame claimed the victory.

Five years later, and following a 40–0 pasting in South Bend the previous year, the Irish traveled to Norman to face a Sooners squad that had not lost since the 1952 meeting in South Bend. The mighty Sooners' 47-game winning streak was the best in the country, and they were huge favorites. Somehow, the Irish, losers of two straight, were able to shut down the Sooners' high-powered offense, holding it scoreless. When Dick Lynch scooted around right end for the first and only score of the game, completing a 20-play, 80-yard drive, Notre Dame had upset one of the best teams in the history of college football, 7–0, and ended Oklahoma's record win streak.

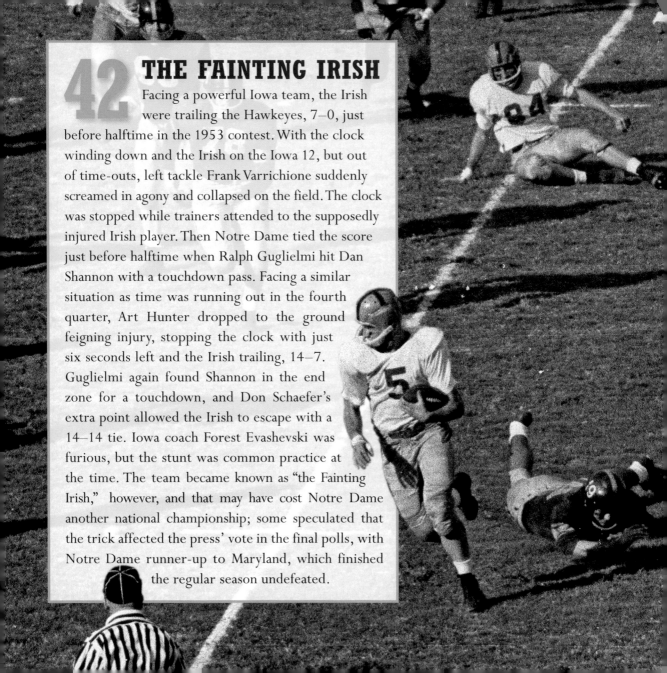

42 THE FAINTING IRISH

Facing a powerful Iowa team, the Irish were trailing the Hawkeyes, 7–0, just before halftime in the 1953 contest. With the clock winding down and the Irish on the Iowa 12, but out of time-outs, left tackle Frank Varrichione suddenly screamed in agony and collapsed on the field. The clock was stopped while trainers attended to the supposedly injured Irish player. Then Notre Dame tied the score just before halftime when Ralph Guglielmi hit Dan Shannon with a touchdown pass. Facing a similar situation as time was running out in the fourth quarter, Art Hunter dropped to the ground feigning injury, stopping the clock with just six seconds left and the Irish trailing, 14–7. Guglielmi again found Shannon in the end zone for a touchdown, and Don Schaefer's extra point allowed the Irish to escape with a 14–14 tie. Iowa coach Forest Evashevski was furious, but the stunt was common practice at the time. The team became known as "the Fainting Irish," however, and that may have cost Notre Dame another national championship; some speculated that the trick affected the press' vote in the final polls, with Notre Dame runner-up to Maryland, which finished the regular season undefeated.

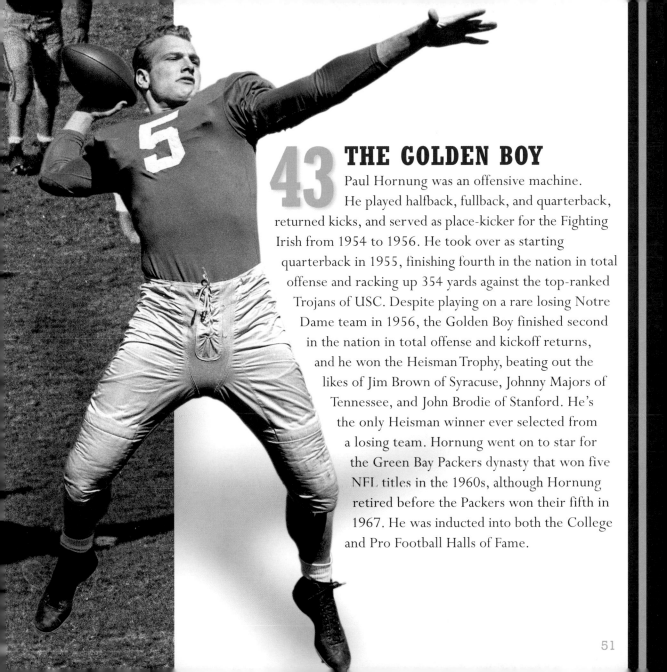

43 THE GOLDEN BOY

Paul Hornung was an offensive machine. He played halfback, fullback, and quarterback, returned kicks, and served as place-kicker for the Fighting Irish from 1954 to 1956. He took over as starting quarterback in 1955, finishing fourth in the nation in total offense and racking up 354 yards against the top-ranked Trojans of USC. Despite playing on a rare losing Notre Dame team in 1956, the Golden Boy finished second in the nation in total offense and kickoff returns, and he won the Heisman Trophy, beating out the likes of Jim Brown of Syracuse, Johnny Majors of Tennessee, and John Brodie of Stanford. He's the only Heisman winner ever selected from a losing team. Hornung went on to star for the Green Bay Packers dynasty that won five NFL titles in the 1960s, although Hornung retired before the Packers won their fifth in 1967. He was inducted into both the College and Pro Football Halls of Fame.

44 SOLID GOLD AND SHAMROCKS

The gold helmets worn by the Fighting Irish mirror the Golden Dome that sits atop Notre Dame's Main Building. They are a college football icon—instantly recognizable. In one of those typical don't-mess-with-perfection moments, Coach Joe Kuharich decided to add a green shamrock to Notre Dame's helmets in 1959. The shamrock remained through 1962 and was replaced by white numerals in 1963. When Ara Parseghian took over as head coach in 1964, he wisely returned to the classic solid gold design, and the helmets have remained unchanged since then.

45 PAINTING THE HELMETS

It is considered a great honor to be selected as one of the student managers responsible for painting Notre Dame's gold helmets. Each Monday preceding a game, the managers spray the helmet of each player dressing for the game with a fresh coat of paint that contains actual gold dust—up to as many as 120 helmets per week.

46 YOUR ATTENTION PLEASE

Tim McCarthy, now retired from the Indiana State Police, has been making safety announcements prior to Notre Dame home games since 1960. He's turned it into an art form, if bad puns are considered an art form. In an effort to curb discourteous and unsafe driving following the games, he has used now classic puns such as "Don't let your day go down the drain by not heeding my silly safety plug" and "No one relishes a pickled driver."

Ara Parseghian celebrates his first victory as Notre Dame head coach after the team's 31–7 victory over Wisconsin on September 26, 1964.

47 ARA PARSEGHIAN

Parseghian had shown Notre Dame just how good a coach he was by beating the Irish four consecutive times from 1959 to 1962 while coaching at Northwestern. When the university decided to make a change following a miserable 2–7 campaign in 1963, it turned to Parseghian even though he was neither a Notre Dame graduate nor a Catholic, as most of the coaches who preceded him were.

Parseghian was a master at getting the most out of his players and maximizing their skills. He turned quarterback John Huarte into a Heisman Trophy winner and end Jack Snow into a first-team All-American in his first season at the helm, as the Irish won their first nine games before falling to USC in the finale, 20–17, after Notre Dame led, 17–3, at halftime. The team gave up only 77 points all year.

Two national championships followed, in 1966 and 1973. In 11 seasons as head coach of the Fighting Irish, Parseghian notched a cumulative record of 95–17–4, including a perfect 11–0 in 1973, capped by a thrilling 24–23 win over Alabama in the Sugar Bowl. Only once in "the Era of Ara" did his team lose more than two games during the regular season. He resigned at the end of the 1974 season. Parseghian was inducted into the College Football Hall of Fame in 1980. A statue in his honor, depicting his players carrying Parseghian off the field following the 1971 Cotton Bowl, stands outside Notre Dame Stadium.

48 HUARTE TO SNOW

In 1964, under first-year coach Ara Parseghian, Huarte exploded on the national scene, passing for 2,062 yards on the season with 16 touchdowns. Taking advantage of Parseghian's wise move to switch halfback Jack Snow to split end, Huarte bested his previous season total by more than 1,800 yards. Snow caught 60 passes totaling 1,114 yards, setting school records with both stats. He was named a first-team All-American, and Huarte won the Heisman Trophy. Only a late touchdown by USC in the final game of the season kept the team from going undefeated and earning consideration for another national championship.

49 ARA, STOP THE SNOW

Snow began to fall during a late-season game in South Bend in 1964, when the student section began to chant, "Ara, stop the snow." Parseghian responded with, "Do you think I could?" A few years later, after winning a national championship, when the chant arose again, he turned to the crowd and cracked, "Do you think I should?"

"A good coach will make his players see what they can be rather than what they are."

—Ara Parseghian

John Huarte and Roger Staubach (Navy) at the 1964 North-South All-Star Game
Inset: Ara Parseghian celebrating Notre Dame's victory in the 1973 Sugar Bowl

50 TOUCHDOWN JESUS

Notre Dame's Hesburgh Library, named for longtime university president Father Theodore M. Hesburgh, stands just beyond the stadium's north end and was completed in 1964. A 134-feet-tall mosaic of Jesus with his arms raised, known as the Word of Life Mural, graces the south-facing facade. Aligned perfectly with the goalpost at the near end of the field, and mirroring the referee's signal for a touchdown, the artwork has become lovingly known as "Touchdown Jesus."

51 FATHER JOYCE

Notre Dame's main athletic facility, the Joyce Center, is named for Father Ned Joyce, the beloved former executive vice president and chief financial officer of the university, who worked hand in hand with university president Father Theodore Hesburgh for 35 years. Father Joyce served as the chairman of the Faculty Board on Athletics and was instrumental in the continued success of Notre Dame's athletic programs and the expansion of their facilities.

"He was ... a man of impeccable moral character, shrewd judgment, rocklike fidelity, and unfailing dependability."

—Father Hesburgh on Father Joyce

52 THE MASCOTS

Dressed in green and gold and wielding a shillelagh, the Notre Dame mascot, a leprechaun, works his magic, leading cheers, inspiring the crowd, and matching points scored with push-ups—all in an attempt to bring home another Irish victory. The leprechaun has been the official mascot of Notre Dame athletics since 1965.

Prior to the adoption of the leprechaun, a series of Irish terriers served as mascot for the Fighting Irish football team. The original terrier was presented to Coach Knute Rockne in 1930 by Charles Otis of Cleveland, and it was known as Brick Top Shuan-Rhu. Several terriers successively filled the role as mascot and were usually given the name Clashmore Mike.

"Who knew the dude from the Lucky Charms commercials could be so feisty?"

—About.com

Left: Johnny Lujack holds Clashmore Mike.
Right: The Fighting Irish leprechaun, with cheerleaders, leads the team onto the field.

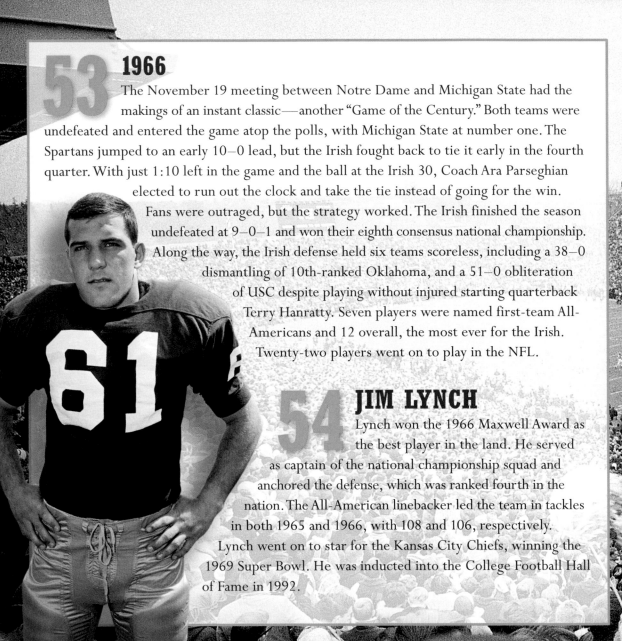

53 1966

The November 19 meeting between Notre Dame and Michigan State had the makings of an instant classic—another "Game of the Century." Both teams were undefeated and entered the game atop the polls, with Michigan State at number one. The Spartans jumped to an early 10–0 lead, but the Irish fought back to tie it early in the fourth quarter. With just 1:10 left in the game and the ball at the Irish 30, Coach Ara Parseghian elected to run out the clock and take the tie instead of going for the win. Fans were outraged, but the strategy worked. The Irish finished the season undefeated at 9–0–1 and won their eighth consensus national championship. Along the way, the Irish defense held six teams scoreless, including a 38–0 dismantling of 10th-ranked Oklahoma, and a 51–0 obliteration of USC despite playing without injured starting quarterback Terry Hanratty. Seven players were named first-team All-Americans and 12 overall, the most ever for the Irish. Twenty-two players went on to play in the NFL.

54 JIM LYNCH

Lynch won the 1966 Maxwell Award as the best player in the land. He served as captain of the national championship squad and anchored the defense, which was ranked fourth in the nation. The All-American linebacker led the team in tackles in both 1965 and 1966, with 108 and 106, respectively. Lynch went on to star for the Kansas City Chiefs, winning the 1969 Super Bowl. He was inducted into the College Football Hall of Fame in 1992.

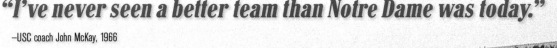

"I've never seen a better team than Notre Dame was today."

—USC coach John McKay, 1966

MICHIGAN STATE Spartans
NOTRE DAME Fighting Irish

SPARTAN
GRIDIRON
NEWS 50¢   *Souvenir Program*   November 19, 1966
SPARTAN STADIUM
Kickoff 1:30 p.m.

55 MR. FLING TO MR. CLING

The combination of sophomore quarterback Terry Hanratty and end Jim Seymour earned this clever nickname in 1966, as the two led Notre Dame to an undefeated season and national championship. In the season opener, Hanratty completed 13 passes to Seymour for 276 yards, a record that still stands, as the Irish defeated Purdue, 26–14. Over the course of three years, the pair set numerous team records. When they graduated, Seymour held the team record for career receptions with 138, and Hanratty was Notre Dame's all-time leader in passing and total offense.

56 THE JUDGES

Alan Page was a three-year starter at defensive end for the Irish and played on the 1966 national championship team, earning consensus All-American honors that year. Bob Thomas was the place-kicker on the 1973 team. His 19-yard field goal with just a few minutes remaining provided the winning margin in a 24–23 victory over top-ranked Alabama in the Sugar Bowl, which won Notre Dame another national championship. Page went on to play 15 seasons in the NFL, with Minnesota and Chicago, and won the league MVP award in 1971—the first defensive player ever to win the award. Thomas spent 12 years in the NFL, mostly with Chicago. Both earned law degrees and went on to become state Supreme Court justices—Page in Minnesota in 1992, and Thomas in Illinois in 2000.

Bob "Rocky" Bleier (28) and Terry Hanratty (5) celebrate Hanratty's touchdown versus California, September 23, 1967.

"Ara let us be us."
–Terry Hanratty

57 JOE THEISMANN

Theismann took over as the team's starting quarterback in his sophomore season, late in 1969, after starter Terry Hanratty was injured. After two wins and a tie, he led the Irish to a near upset of Texas in the Cotton Bowl, in Notre Dame's first bowl appearance in 45 years. The following year, Theismann led his team to nine straight victories before losing, 38–28, to USC in a torrential downpour. Despite the horrible conditions, he set the Notre Dame record for passing yards in a game, with 526 yards—a record that still stands—and set single-season team records for passing yardage (2,429) and touchdowns (16). The Irish finished number two in the polls that year and avenged the previous year's loss to Texas in the Cotton Bowl with a 24–11 victory, ending the Longhorns' 30-game winning streak. Theismann was named first-team All-American. He broke his own season passing and touchdown records in 1971, and over the course of his Notre Dame career, he compiled a 20–3–2 record as a starting quarterback, throwing for 4,411 yards and 31 touchdowns. Theismann played for Toronto in the Canadian Football League for three years before moving to the Washington Redskins in 1974. He spent 12 years in Washington, winning a Super Bowl championship in 1983. Theismann was inducted into the College Football Hall of Fame in 2003.

58 THEISMANN RHYMES WITH HEISMAN

At the urging of longtime Notre Dame sports information director Roger Valdiserri, in an effort to promote his candidacy for the Heisman Trophy, Joe Theismann changed the pronunciation of his last name from "Theez-man" to rhyme with "Heisman." During Theismann's senior season, the sports information office continually ran out the slogan "Theismann, as in Heisman," in an effort to help him win the coveted award. He finished second to Stanford's Jim Plunkett.

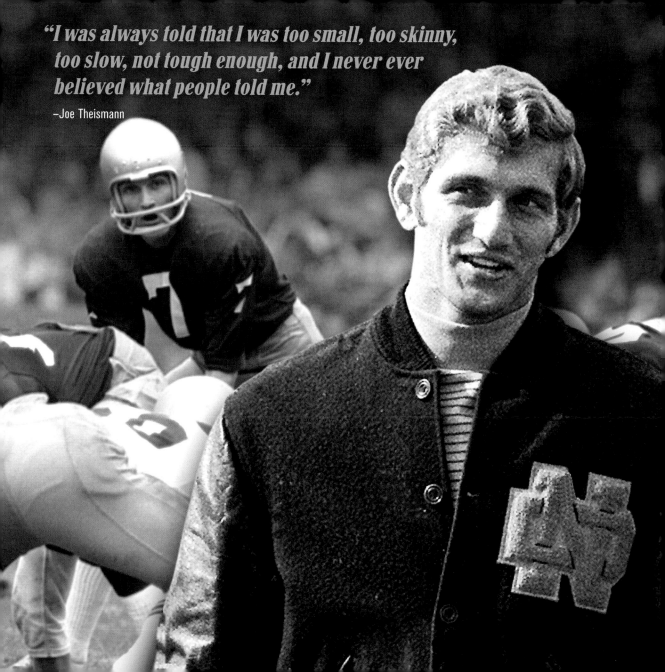

> "*I was always told that I was too small, too skinny, too slow, not tough enough, and I never ever believed what people told me.*"
>
> –Joe Theismann

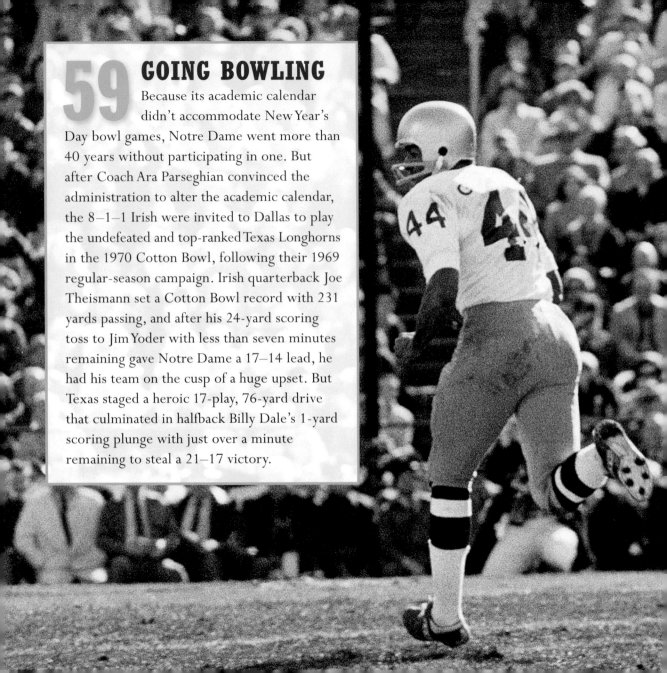

59 GOING BOWLING

Because its academic calendar didn't accommodate New Year's Day bowl games, Notre Dame went more than 40 years without participating in one. But after Coach Ara Parseghian convinced the administration to alter the academic calendar, the 8–1–1 Irish were invited to Dallas to play the undefeated and top-ranked Texas Longhorns in the 1970 Cotton Bowl, following their 1969 regular-season campaign. Irish quarterback Joe Theismann set a Cotton Bowl record with 231 yards passing, and after his 24-yard scoring toss to Jim Yoder with less than seven minutes remaining gave Notre Dame a 17–14 lead, he had his team on the cusp of a huge upset. But Texas staged a heroic 17-play, 76-yard drive that culminated in halfback Billy Dale's 1-yard scoring plunge with just over a minute remaining to steal a 21–17 victory.

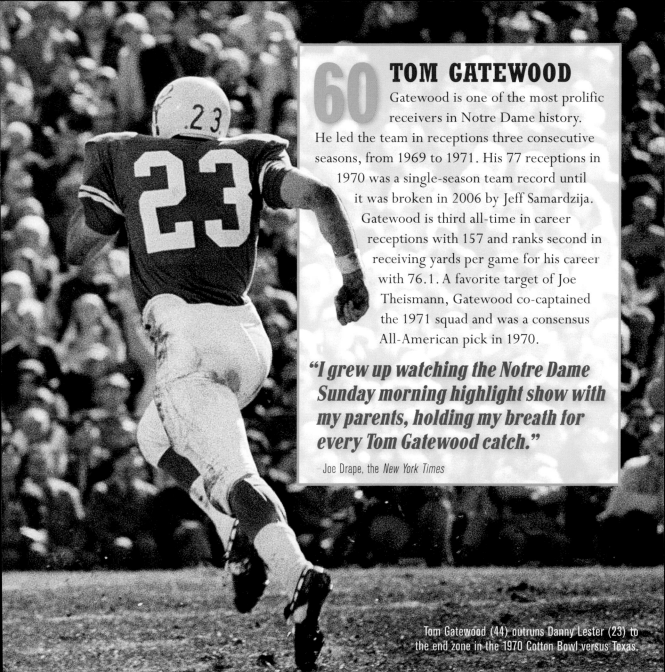

60 TOM GATEWOOD

Gatewood is one of the most prolific receivers in Notre Dame history. He led the team in receptions three consecutive seasons, from 1969 to 1971. His 77 receptions in 1970 was a single-season team record until it was broken in 2006 by Jeff Samardzija. Gatewood is third all-time in career receptions with 157 and ranks second in receiving yards per game for his career with 76.1. A favorite target of Joe Theismann, Gatewood co-captained the 1971 squad and was a consensus All-American pick in 1970.

"I grew up watching the Notre Dame Sunday morning highlight show with my parents, holding my breath for every Tom Gatewood catch."

—Joe Drape, the *New York Times*

Tom Gatewood (44) outruns Danny Lester (23) to the end zone in the 1970 Cotton Bowl versus Texas.

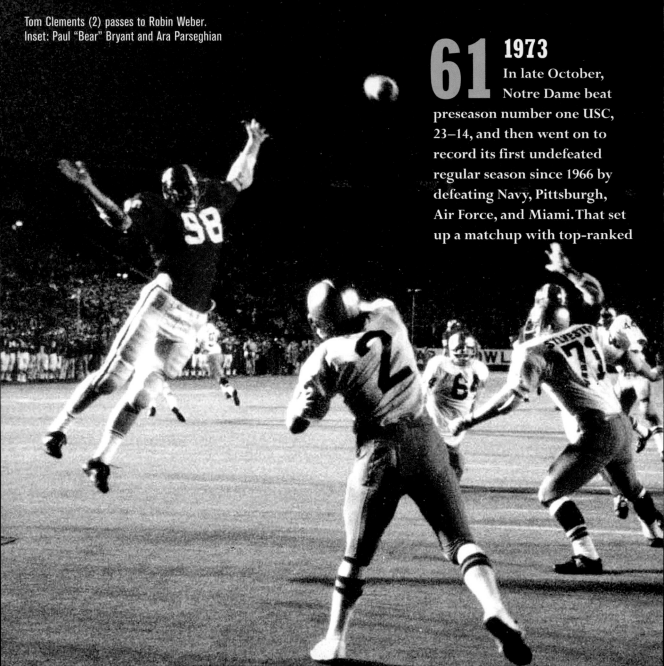

Tom Clements (2) passes to Robin Weber.
Inset: Paul "Bear" Bryant and Ara Parseghian

61 1973

In late October, Notre Dame beat preseason number one USC, 23–14, and then went on to record its first undefeated regular season since 1966 by defeating Navy, Pittsburgh, Air Force, and Miami. That set up a matchup with top-ranked and undefeated Alabama in the Sugar Bowl. It was the first meeting ever between the two football powers, coached by legends Ara Parseghian and Alabama's Paul "Bear" Bryant. Freshman Al Hunter returned a kickoff 93 yards for a touchdown to give Notre Dame a 14–7 lead, but the game continued to seesaw back and forth deep into the fourth quarter. The Crimson Tide took the lead, 23–21, but a missed extra point proved to be its undoing. The Irish drove deep into Alabama territory, where a 19-yard Bob Thomas field goal put them up, 24–23, in the final minutes. After stopping 'Bama and forcing a punt, Notre Dame had the ball deep in its own territory, desperate to run out the clock. On third down, quarterback Tom Clements dropped back into his own end zone and found reserve Robin Weber for a 35-yard gain and a first down that allowed Notre Dame to keep the ball and secure its ninth national championship.

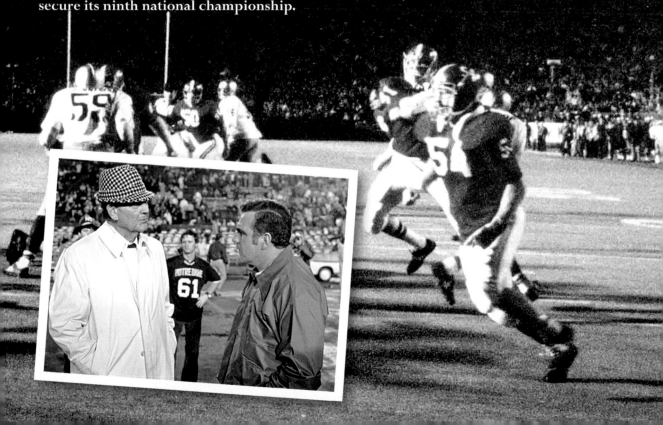

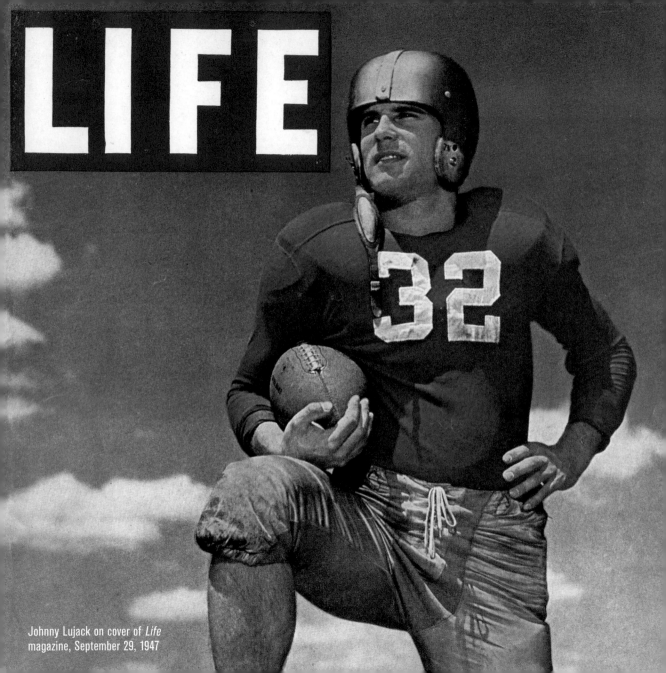

LIFE

Johnny Lujack on cover of *Life*
magazine, September 29, 1947

62 DAN DEVINE

When Coach Ara Parseghian retired following the Irish's 13–11 win over Alabama in the 1974 Orange Bowl, Notre Dame had some big shoes to fill. Enter Dan Devine, former coach at Arizona State, Missouri, and most recently, the NFL's Green Bay Packers. He had been a leading candidate for the job back in 1964 when Parseghian was hired. Even though Devine led the team to six consecutive winning seasons, with a combined record of 53–16–1, four bowl appearances with three victories, and Notre Dame's 10th national championship in 1977, he was never fully embraced and loved by the fans like his predecessor. Devine oversaw the development of quarterback Joe Montana during his tenure and reaped the benefits of Montana's propensity for dramatic comebacks. Devine retired at the conclusion of the 1980 season and was inducted into the College Football Hall of Fame in 1985.

63 THE BLUE AND GOLD

Notre Dame's original colors were yellow and blue. Yellow represented light and blue truth. The switch was made from yellow to gold after the dome and statue of St. Mary atop the Main Building were painted gold.

64 GREEN JERSEYS

Coach Dan Devine introduced the now-beloved green jerseys for the 1977 game against Southern Cal. Notre Dame demolished the Trojans, 49–19. Fans loved the new look and embraced it immediately. While some Irish teams have worn green for every home game, the jerseys are currently worn only for "special occasions." The 1977 game wasn't the first time Notre Dame had worn green. Way back in the early years of Knute Rockne, the Irish often wore green jerseys to distinguish themselves from an opponent wearing blue. Rockne was also known to use the color as a psychological ploy, once starting his second string in the traditional navy blue, then sending out the first string in green jerseys after falling behind Navy, 6–0. The Irish went on to win, 19–6. The green jerseys were also popular during Coach Frank Leahy's tenure. Johnny Lujack was featured on the cover of *Life* magazine sporting the bright green.

65 RUDY

All he ever wanted was to play football for Notre Dame, but at 5 feet 7 inches and 165 pounds, Daniel Ruettiger didn't draw any interest from the elite football program. After spending two years at Holy Cross, "Rudy" finally got his wish, gaining acceptance to the university and earning a walk-on role with the football team's practice squad. In the final home game of Rudy's senior season in 1975, versus Georgia Tech, head coach Dan Devine allowed Rudy to dress for the game and inserted him in the last two plays—the only two of Rudy's career at Notre Dame. Like something out of Hollywood, Rudy sacked the Yellow Jackets' quarterback on the game's final play and was carried off the field by his teammates. His story became the stuff movies are made of. The film *Rudy*, starring Sean Astin in the lead role, was produced and released in 1993, serving as inspiration to underdogs and dreamers everywhere.

66 BY THE NUMBERS

Despite the lengthy list of Irish greats, Notre Dame has never retired a jersey number. However, the history and tradition of each number are recognized when players are given their jerseys. Each player receives a card listing the notable predecessors who have worn the number they share. Perhaps the most famous number in Irish football history is number 3, which was worn by Ralph Guglielmi, George Izo, Daryle Lamonica, Coley O'Brien, Joe Montana, Rick Mirer, and Ron Powlus. Elmer Layden, Paul Hornung, and Terry Hanratty wore number 5. And number 7 has been worn by Irish legends John Huarte, Joe Theismann, Steve Beuerlein, and Jarious Jackson.

67 FIRST TO 1,000

It's hard to believe, with all the legendary ball carriers Notre Dame has had in its historic past, that it wasn't until 1976 that one finally rushed for more than 1,000 yards in a season. Al Hunter was that back, notching 1,058 yards.

Al Hunter (25) looks for a hole versus USC.

Joe Montana (3) prepares to pass versus USC.

68 JOE MONTANA

His is a household name these days, synonymous with thrilling comebacks, but Montana's college career started somewhat less conspicuously. As a freshman, Montana was a seventh-string quarterback relegated to spot duty in freshman team games. In his sophomore season, he came on to engineer two consecutive stunning fourth-quarter comebacks versus North Carolina and Air Force, and people started to take notice. But a shoulder injury sidelined him for the entire 1976 season, and when the 1977 season began, Montana was listed as the third quarterback on the team's depth chart. After a benching of first-stringer Rusty Lisch and a career-ending injury to backup Gary Forystek, Montana took over the starting role during the third game and led his team to nine straight wins and a national title. In his senior year of 1978, Montana and the Irish posted a record of 9–3 with a spectacular come-from-behind 35–34 win over Houston in the Cotton Bowl. He went on to become a football legend during his pro career with the San Francisco 49ers, winning four Super Bowl titles and three Super Bowl MVP awards.

"Winners, I am convinced, imagine their dreams first. They want it with all their heart and expect it to come true. There is, I believe, no other way to live."

– Joe Montana

Joe Montana and Dan Devine confer on the sidelines during the 1979 Cotton Bowl, also known as "the Ice Bowl."

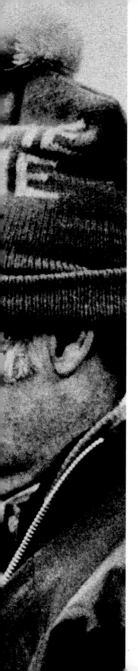

69 JOE'S COMEBACKS

In his six greatest comebacks, Montana and the Irish put up 114 points in less than 37 minutes of game time:

- 1975: Trailed UNC, 14–6, with 5:11 left, and won, 21–14, on an 80-yard completion to Tom Burgmeier
- 1975: Trailed Air Force, 30–10, with 13:00 left, and won, 31–30
- 1977: Trailed Purdue, 24–14, with 11:00 left, and won, 31–24
- 1978: Trailed Pitt, 17–7, with 13:46 left, and won, 26–17
- 1978: Trailed USC, 24–6, with 12:59 left, took the lead, 25–24, with just 45 seconds remaining, but a USC field goal gave the Trojans the win, 27–25. Montana threw for a career-best 358 yards.

And then there was what is probably his best and most dramatic comeback, the 1979 Cotton Bowl against Houston—the game that became known as "the Chicken Soup Game." It was a frigid day in ice-encrusted Dallas. Montana, suffering from the flu and hypothermia, huddled under wool blankets and ate chicken soup to warm himself during halftime. When the second half began, Montana remained in the locker room. But with less than eight minutes left in the game, trailing, 34–12, he returned to the field. Tom Belden got Notre Dame's comeback started with a 33-yard return of a blocked punt for a touchdown. Montana then engineered a 61-yard scoring drive, and the two-point conversion made it 34–28 with 4:15 remaining. With only 28 seconds left, the Irish got one last chance, stopping the Cougars on downs at their own 29. After throwing the ball out of bounds to stop the clock with six seconds left, Montana found Kris Haines in the end zone from 8 yards out for a game-tying touchdown. Joe Unis' point after gave Notre Dame an unbelievable 35–34 win.

70 ROSS BROWNER

Browner was one of the best defensive players ever to don the blue and gold of Notre Dame. A four-year starter, he played on teams that won national championships in 1973 and 1977, posting a 39–7 record over that time. The standout defensive end was a two-time unanimous All-American in 1976 and 1977, and his 340 tackles are the all-time Notre Dame record for a defensive lineman. The leader of some of the best defensive teams in Fighting Irish history, Browner won the Outland Trophy as the nation's best lineman in 1976. He followed that up with the Lombardi Trophy for the nation's best lineman and the Maxwell Award as college football's best player in 1977, when he also finished fifth in Heisman Trophy voting. Browner spent nine years in the NFL with the Cincinnati Bengals and one with the Green Bay Packers. He was inducted into the College Football Hall of Fame in 1999.

LOMBARDI AWARD
OUTSTANDING
COLLEGE LINEMAN

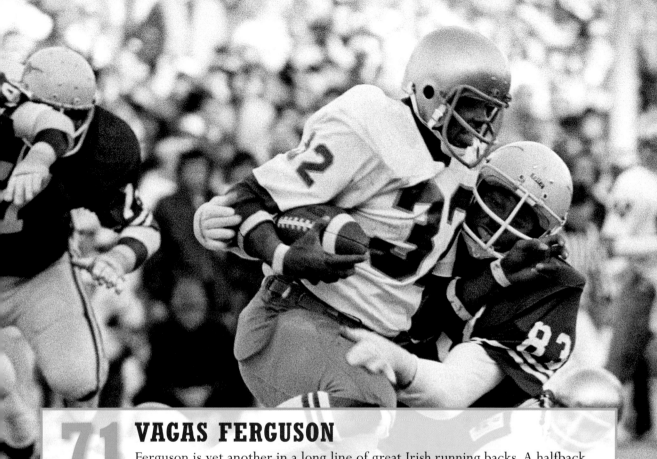

71 VAGAS FERGUSON

Ferguson is yet another in a long line of great Irish running backs. A halfback, Ferguson played for Notre Dame from 1976 to 1979 and was a key member of the 1977 national championship team, running for 100 yards and three touchdowns in the 1978 Cotton Bowl. He was the first Irish back to rush for more than 1,000 yards in consecutive seasons, in 1978 and 1979, setting the all-time Notre Dame single-season rushing mark in 1979 with 1,437 yards. Ferguson's 255 yards rushing in 1978 versus Georgia Tech set an Irish single-game record, which was broken by Julius Jones (262 yards) in 2003. He went on to spend four years in the NFL, with New England, Houston, and Cleveland.

Bob Crable leaps over teammates to block a field goal attempt by Michigan's Bryan Virgil.

72 CRABLE'S BLOCK

A linebacker, Bob Crable holds the Notre Dame record for tackles in a game (26), in a season (187 in 1979), and for his career (521). He was an All-American in both 1980 and 1981. But perhaps his most memorable moment with Notre Dame came in the 1979 matchup with Michigan. Notre Dame led, 12–10, with just six seconds left in the game. Michigan set up for a game-winning field goal attempt. Crable lined up a couple of steps behind the defensive line, and when the ball was snapped, he stepped up on the back of a teammate and leaped over the line to block the kick and save the game for Notre Dame.

73 KEN MacAFEE

MacAfee, a three-time All-American, played on the national championship team in 1977, setting a single-season record for catches by a tight end with 54. He was selected as the Walter Camp Player of the Year—the first lineman to receive the award—and finished third in the Heisman Trophy voting. His 128 career receptions are also a team record for tight ends. MacAfee went on to play with the San Francisco 49ers in the NFL. He was inducted into the College Football Hall of Fame in 1997.

74 THE DAY THE WIND DIED

On September 20, 1980, with Notre Dame trailing 14th-ranked Michigan, 27–26, kicker Harry Oliver came on to attempt a 51-yard field goal with just seconds remaining in the game. Holder Tim Koegel placed the ball down and Oliver, kicking into a wind that had been gusting between 15 and 20 miles per hour all afternoon, drilled the kick through the uprights as time expired for a 29–27 Irish victory. Koegel claims the wind died just as Oliver was making the kick. Tony Roberts' radio call of the play is legendary.

75 ON THE MIKE

Mike Collins is the voice of Notre Dame Stadium. The 1967 Notre Dame graduate took over for Frank Crosiar in 1982. He got his start as the public address announcer at Notre Dame hockey games in the late 1970s. Crosiar spent 34 years in the booth prior to Collins' arrival, calling 170 consecutive games from 1948 through 1981.

76 GERRY FAUST

He wasn't the most successful Irish football coach ever. In fact, he's considered by many to be one of the least successful. However, it is worth noting that when Notre Dame officials chose to name Faust as successor to Dan Devine, his only previous coaching experience had been with Archbishop Moeller High School in Cincinnati, where he had led his teams to a 174–17–2 record over 18 years, including five Ohio state AAA titles in six years, from 1975 to 1980. Faust's teams went 30–26–1 in five seasons at Notre Dame.

"I'd loved Notre Dame as long as I can remember."

—Gerry Faust, from *The Golden Dream*

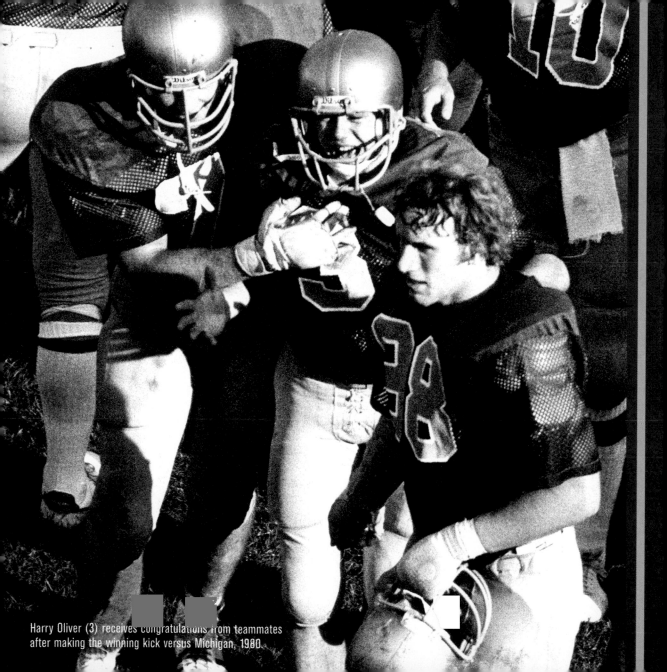

Harry Oliver (3) receives congratulations from teammates after making the winning kick versus Michigan, 1980.

77 ALLEN PINKETT

Although the Gerry Faust years are viewed as a down time in Irish football history, Pinkett was a standout running back on mediocre teams. Pinkett was the first Irish back to surpass 1,000 yards in three consecutive seasons, from 1983 to 1985, and set the all-time record for total rushing yards with 4,131, later broken by Autry Denson. The two-time All-American is Notre Dame's career scoring leader, with 320 points on 53 touchdowns and a two-point conversion, and is tied with Vagas Ferguson for the most rushing touchdowns in a season with 17.

78 AMERICAN GLADIATORS

Former Notre Dame stars Vagas Ferguson and Allen Pinkett were pitted against former USC stars Anthony Davis and Charles White in an episode of *American Gladiators* broadcast in 1995.

Allen Pinkett

79 THE FIXER

Lou Holtz, aka "the Fixer," took over the head coaching duties in 1986, replacing Gerry Faust. Holtz had successfully turned around programs at William & Mary, North Carolina State, Arkansas, and Minnesota, and Notre Dame needed him to work his magic in South Bend. One of Holtz' first moves was to make kick returner Tim Brown a flanker, adding his big-play capabilities to the offense. The Irish struggled in Holtz' first season, losing four of the first five games, but the turnaround was already under way. Over the course of 11 years in South Bend, Holtz' Irish teams won 100 games, losing only 30, with two ties. The 100 wins make Holtz the second-winningest coach in Notre Dame history, behind Knute Rockne's 105. In just his third season, the Irish went undefeated and beat West Virginia in the Fiesta Bowl, 34–21, to win Notre Dame's 11th national title. It was the second of nine straight New Year's Day bowl appearances by the Irish. Holtz' teams also finished the year ranked sixth or higher five times.

80 PLAY LIKE A CHAMPION TODAY

Coach Holtz came across this quote in a book he was reading about the history of Notre Dame. Inspired by its message, Holtz had a sign with the quote installed on the wall above the stairs that the players take as they leave the locker room and head up the tunnel to the field at Notre Dame Stadium. Since its installation, players have made it a tradition to slap the sign as they pass under it.

81 THE SCULPTOR

A statue honoring Lou Holtz, created by Notre Dame grad Jerry McKenna, was unveiled in 2008, inside Gate D of Notre Dame Stadium. It joins other works by McKenna of famed football coaches, including Knute Rockne, Frank Leahy, and Ara Parseghian.

Lou Holtz

82 TIM BROWN

The great Tim Brown had an inauspicious start to his Notre Dame career, fumbling the opening kickoff of the 1984 season in a 23–21 loss to Purdue. Things only got better and better from there. Coach Holtz also played Brown—a consistent big-play threat as a kick and punt returner—as a back and receiver, highlighting his incredible speed and agility. His all-purpose yards totals of 1,937 in 1986 and 1,847 in 1987 still top the Notre Dame record books. Brown twice earned All-American honors, in 1986 and 1987, and also won the Heisman Trophy in 1987, making him the first wide receiver ever to win the award. He went on to a highly successful career in the NFL with Oakland and Tampa Bay.

"What made my five years at Notre Dame special were all the great young men we recruited, like Tim Brown. I was blessed."

–Gerry Faust, from *Gerry Faust's Tales from the Notre Dame Sideline*

TIM BROWN

83 CATHOLICS VERSUS CONVICTS

The slogan first appeared on T-shirts printed by a Notre Dame student prior to the October 15 slugfest with the University of Miami, in 1988. While the Catholic reference is obvious, the term "Convicts" disparagingly referred to the Hurricanes' propensity for on- and off-field shenanigans. The game pitted two undefeated teams—the top-ranked Hurricanes, with their 36-game regular-season winning streak, and the fourth-ranked Irish, who had been annihilated by Miami in their previous four meetings by a combined score of 133–20.

The Irish defense was ferocious, forcing seven Miami turnovers, and the offense, led by Tony Rice and Raghib Ismail, more than held its own. Notre Dame led, 31–24, with about seven minutes left in the game, when Irish safety George Streeter forced a Cleveland Gary fumble at the Notre Dame 1, and Michael Stonebreaker recovered to preserve the lead. But with only a couple of minutes remaining, a Tony Rice fumble gave the Hurricanes the ball back at the Notre Dame 21. On fourth-and-6 from the 11, quarterback Steve Walsh found Andre Brown for a touchdown. Trailing by 1, Miami coach Jimmy Johnson elected to go for two points and the win. Walsh lofted a pass toward Leonard Conley, but Notre Dame's Pat Terrell stepped in front of Conley and batted the ball away. When Anthony Johnson fell on the ensuing onside kick, Notre Dame had secured a stunning 31–30 victory. The game is considered by many to be the greatest victory in Notre Dame history.

Chris Zorich (50) makes a tackle versus Miami, 1988.

84 THE THREE AMIGOS

Wes Pritchett, Michael Stonebreaker, and Frank Stams made up the trio of linebackers known as "the Three Amigos," terrorizing opposing offenses and leading Notre Dame to a 12–0 record and the 1988 national championship. Stams and Stonebreaker were named first-team All-Americans.

85 CHRIS ZORICH

Originally a linebacker, the incredibly strong and swift Zorich was moved to nose tackle during his freshman season, but he rode the bench the entire year. Finally given the chance to play as a sophomore, Zorich made the most of it, earning first-team All-American honors (Newspaper Enterprise Association) while helping lead the team to the 1988 national championship. Zorich won consensus All-American honors in 1989 and 1990 as well, and he was named the nation's top linebacker in 1990, winning the Lombardi Award. Zorich spent seven years in the NFL with the Chicago Bears and the Washington Redskins. He was inducted into the College Football Hall of Fame in 2007.

"He's one of the greatest nose guards we've played against."

–Penn State coach Joe Paterno on Chris Zorich

86 THE ROCKET

Raghib "Rocket" Ismail wasn't big. In fact, he was small by football standards at only 5 feet 10 inches and 175 pounds. But he was fast. Real fast. As a freshman, Ismail earned a starting position on the 1988 national championship squad and was named All-American in each of the next two seasons, finishing second in the 1990 Heisman Trophy voting and winning the Walter Camp Player of the Year award. Twice Ismail returned two kickoffs for touchdowns in a game, in 1988 versus Rice and in 1989 versus Michigan. In the 1990 meeting between Notre Dame and Miami, Ismail returned a kickoff 94 yards for a touchdown, keying the 29–20 Irish victory over the second-ranked Hurricanes.

Following a successful career in the CFL and the NFL, the former Notre Dame star participated in *Ty Murray's Celebrity Bull Riding Challenge*, a six-episode series that was broadcast on CMT in 2007. Commenting on the experience, Ismail said, "On the bull, I felt like, you know, lost in space, man. It was just ridiculous."

87 JEROME BETTIS

"The Bus" is better known for his success in the NFL with the Pittsburgh Steelers, but before that, he was an often unstoppable force at Notre Dame. In three seasons at starting fullback for the Irish, Bettis racked up more than 1,900 yards rushing, leading the team in rushing yards in 1991 with 972. Bettis rushed for 150 yards, scoring three touchdowns in the fourth quarter of Notre Dame's 39–28 upset win over Florida in the 1992 Sugar Bowl, and was named the game's MVP.

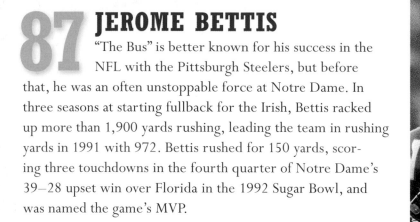

88 CHEERIOS

Prior to the 1992 Sugar Bowl in which Notre Dame faced third-ranked Florida, a waiter in Friday's asked Lou Holtz, "What's the difference between Notre Dame and Cheerios? Cheerios belong in a bowl." Holtz used the joke to motivate his team to a 39–28 upset win, after trailing 16–7 at halftime.

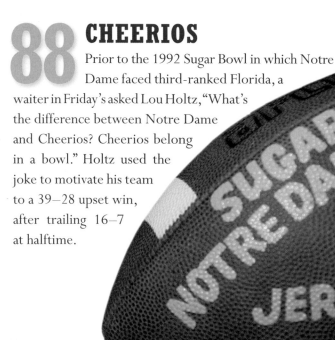

Jerome Bettis rushes for a touchdown against Northwestern University.

89 REGGIE BROOKS

Brooks' 20-yard touchdown run through the Michigan defense, in which he broke no fewer than five tackles, won the ESPN 1992 Play of the Year. Brooks rushed for 1,343 yards that season, averaging 8.04 yards per carry, second only to George Gipp's 8.10 average in 1920.

90 THE SNOW BOWL

On November 14, 1992, trailing Penn State 16–9 with 4:19 to play in a swirling snowstorm in South Bend, quarterback Rick Mirer drove the Irish to the Penn State 3 with 25 seconds left. Jerome Bettis caught a Mirer pass for a touchdown to cut the lead to one. Then Coach Holtz decided to go for two and the win. With an empty backfield, Mirer waited what must have seemed like forever to Irish fans before scrambling right and finding tailback Reggie Brooks in the right corner of the end zone for the game-winning two-point conversion. Brooks, at 5 feet 8 inches, was the smallest player on the field and had only one reception all season. The crowd was delirious with joy.

Reggie Brooks on his way to a 73-yard touchdown versus Boston College, 1992

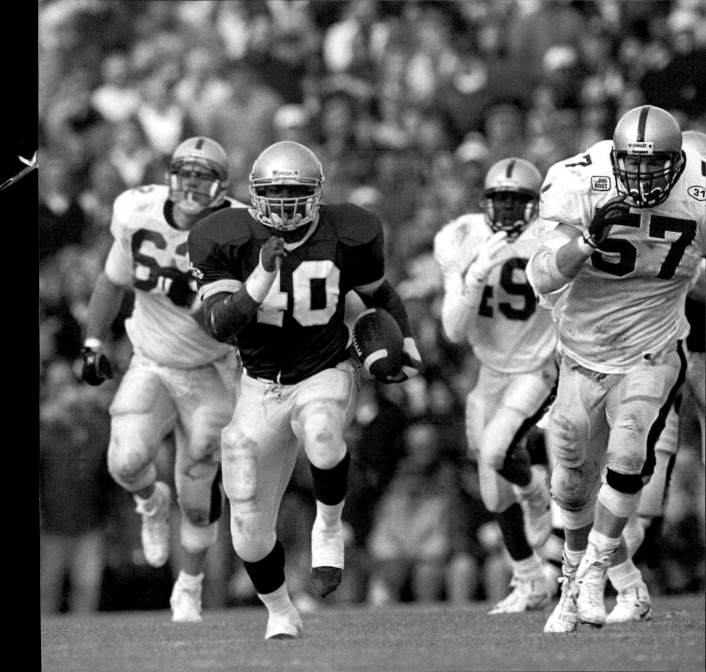

91 YET ANOTHER GAME OF THE CENTURY

Perhaps the phrase "Game of the Century" is a bit overused, but this contest actually lived up to the pregame hype. On November 13, 1993, Florida State and Notre Dame met in South Bend in a late-season battle of unbeatens. Florida State sat atop the polls at number one, and Notre Dame was number two. Both teams boasted 16-game winning streaks. Florida State went up, 7–0, early, but Notre Dame answered and led, 21–7, at halftime. The Irish remained in control for much of the game, but after the Seminoles had cut the lead to seven points with 10:40 to play, Irish quarterback Kevin McDougal led an 80-yard drive that put Notre Dame up, 31–17, seemingly giving the team control again with just a few minutes remaining. Florida State came right back, though, scoring with just 1:39 left in the game, again cutting the lead to seven. After the Irish went three and out, failing to run out the clock, the Seminoles got one last chance with 51 seconds left. They quickly moved from their own 37 to the Irish 14 with 10 seconds remaining. Defensive end Thomas Knight knocked down Seminole quarterback Charlie Ward's first attempt, and with three seconds left, defensive back Shawn Wooden batted away Ward's last-gasp pass to Kevin Knox, preserving an inspiring 31–24 victory. The crowd erupted and swarmed the field, celebrating Notre Dame's return to the top— though it wouldn't last.

Fans celebrate Notre Dame's victory over Florida State, 1993. Inset: Irish teammates Mark Zataveski, left, and Mike McGill

Irish players react after David Gordon's 41-yard field goal gave Boston College a 41–39 win over Notre Dame, 1993.

92 THE HOLY WAR

On November 20, 1993, senior quarterback Kevin McDougal engineered one of the greatest Irish comebacks of all time, except...

Top-ranked and undefeated Notre Dame, playing with a bit of a hangover from the Florida State game the previous week, trailed Boston College, 38–17, with just over 11 minutes left in the game. McDougal led the Irish on touchdown-scoring drives of 57, 67, and 66 yards, the last score coming on a fourth-and-goal pass to Lake Dawson with just over a minute left. The extra point gave Notre Dame a 39–38 lead. Boston College got the ball back and drove to the Notre Dame 24; then the Eagles' David Gordon made a 41-yard field goal as time expired to crush Notre Dame's hopes of a perfect season. The Irish went on to defeat Texas A&M, 24–21, in the Cotton Bowl, but finished second in the polls behind Florida State, even though Notre Dame had defeated the Seminoles in November.

"The stars were aligned for them. They played a great game to beat us."

—Kevin McDougal on the Boston College game, from Rivals.com

Reggie Bush (5) helps push Matt Leinart (11) across the
goal line for the winning score versus Notre Dame, 2005.
Inset: Julius Jones

93 JULIUS JONES

Jones led Notre Dame in rushing in 2000, 2001, and 2003, and he set a single-game record at Pittsburgh in his senior year when he rushed for 262 yards in just 24 attempts. He gained more than 200 yards three times that season, also eclipsing the mark against Navy and Stanford. His career total of 2,104 return yards is Notre Dame's all-time highest, surpassing the great Tim Brown's mark of 2,089 yards set from 1984 to 1987. Jones has since gone on to a successful career in the NFL with the Dallas Cowboys and Seattle Seahawks.

94 THE BUSH PUSH

Even though it ultimately ended in defeat for Notre Dame, the October 15, 2005, contest in South Bend versus top-ranked and defending national champion Southern Cal ranks as one of the greatest games in Notre Dame history. The Trojans came in with a gaudy 27-game winning streak, and they led, 28–24, with five minutes left to play. The Irish then drove 87 yards, with quarterback Brady Quinn scoring from 5 yards out with 2:04 left on the clock to take a 31–28 lead. USC got the ball back at its own 25 but faced a fourth-and-9 at its own 26 with time winding down. Quarterback Matt Leinart found Dwayne Jarrett on a fade route down the sideline that resulted in a 61-yard gain to the Irish 13. A couple of runs got the Trojans to the Irish 2. Leinart then scrambled toward the sideline, where a bruising hit by linebacker Corey Mays flipped Leinart and the ball out of bounds at the 1 with three seconds remaining. USC Coach Pete Carroll elected to go for the touchdown and the win, calling for a quarterback sneak. Leinart dove for the goal line but was stopped short by the Irish defense and didn't initially get across. Reggie Bush came in from behind and gave Leinart a push. The shove got him over the line, and USC came away with a stunning and unforgettable 34–31 win.

95 BRADY QUINN

Dorais, Bertelli, Lujack, Huarte, Hanratty, Theismann, and Montana—a who's who of great college quarterbacks who played for Notre Dame. But none of them comes close to the numbers Brady Quinn put up during his four years in South Bend, between 2003 and 2006. Quinn set career marks in passing yards (11,762), yards per game (240), touchdown passes (95), pass completions (929), and lowest interception percentage (2.43). His 3,919 yards passing in 2005 is the all-time Notre Dame season record, and his 37 touchdown passes in 2006 is also a team record. Among his single-game records, Quinn's six touchdown passes versus Brigham Young in 2005 stand out. He was a third-team AP All-American in 2005, and second-team in 2006, when Quinn finished third in Heisman Trophy balloting. He won the Maxwell Award that year and the Johnny Unitas Golden Arm Award for the best college quarterback. Quinn currently plays quarterback for the Cleveland Browns in the NFL.

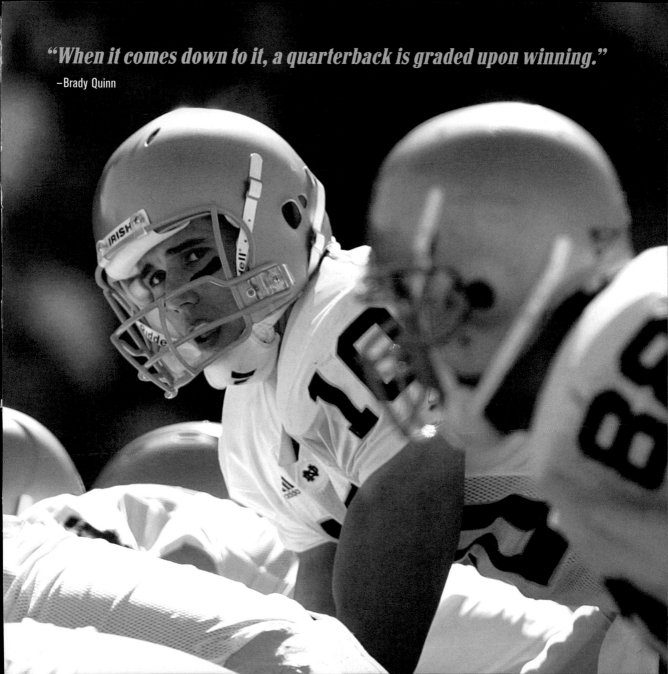

"When it comes down to it, a quarterback is graded upon winning."
–Brady Quinn

96 JEFF SAMARDZIJA

Gus Dorais had Knute Rockne. Terry Hanratty had Jim Seymour. Brady Quinn had Jeff Samardzija A standout pitcher on the Fighting Irish baseball team, Samardzija spent two years as a backup before also emerging as a football star. He soon became Quinn's go-to guy, making 77 receptions for 1,249 yards with 15 touchdowns in 2005. Samardzija caught 78 more passes in 2006 for 1,017 yards and another 12 touchdowns. His 78 catches in 2006 are a school record, as is his career total of 179, and his 2,593 career receiving yards are also the best in Notre Dame history. Since leaving Notre Dame, Samardzija has pursued a career in baseball, and in 2008 he made his first major league appearance, with the Chicago Cubs.

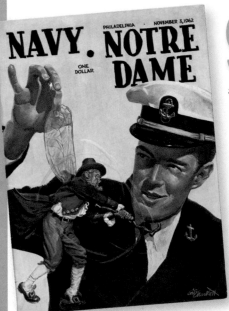

97 THE STREAK

The long-standing rivalry between Notre Dame and Navy dates all the way back to 1927. Since that time, the two teams have played each other more than 80 times, never missing a year. Notre Dame has dominated the series, winning 43 games in a row from 1964 through 2006. Navy ended the streak in dramatic fashion with a 46–44 triple-overtime victory in 2007.

Jeff Samardzija

98 FRIDAY NIGHT PEP RALLIES

They're an institution at Notre Dame. The marching band winds its way through campus to the Joyce Center, where the pep rallies are held. Students pack the center. Coaches, select players, and special guests speak, all in prelude to the big game—and at Notre Dame, every game is a big game.

99 GAME DAY

No event is bigger at Notre Dame: those fleeting, all-too-few Saturdays in autumn when the Fighting Irish host a game at Notre Dame Stadium. The campus is alive with energy. Tailgaters fill the air with the familiar aromas of burgers, brats, and dogs grilling, while dorm barbecues cater to those who aren't part of a tailgate party. As game time approaches, the stadium fills to capacity. The Irish Guard lead the marching band onto the field, and the roar of the crowd becomes deafening as the cheerleaders and the flag-waving leprechaun lead the team onto the field. In South Bend, football is a celebration, and game days are sacrosanct.

Left: Players celebrate a 23–21 victory over Purdue, 2000.
Inset: Coeds cheer at a pep rally.

100 TEN HALL OF FAMERS

In addition to boasting seven Heisman Trophy winners, and 48 members of the College Football Hall of Fame, Notre Dame has had 10 players who later earned induction into the Pro Football Hall of Fame. They are: Curly Lambeau (1963), John McNally (1963), George Trafton (1964), Wayne Millner (1968), George Connor (1975), Paul Hornung (1986), Alan Page (1988), Joe Montana (2000), Nick Buoniconti (2001), and Dave Casper (2002).

Large image: Paul Hornung intercepting a pass versus Indiana, 1955.
Inset (left to right, top to bottom): Lambeau, McNally, Trafton, Millner, Connor, Hornung, Page, Montana, Buoniconti, Casper

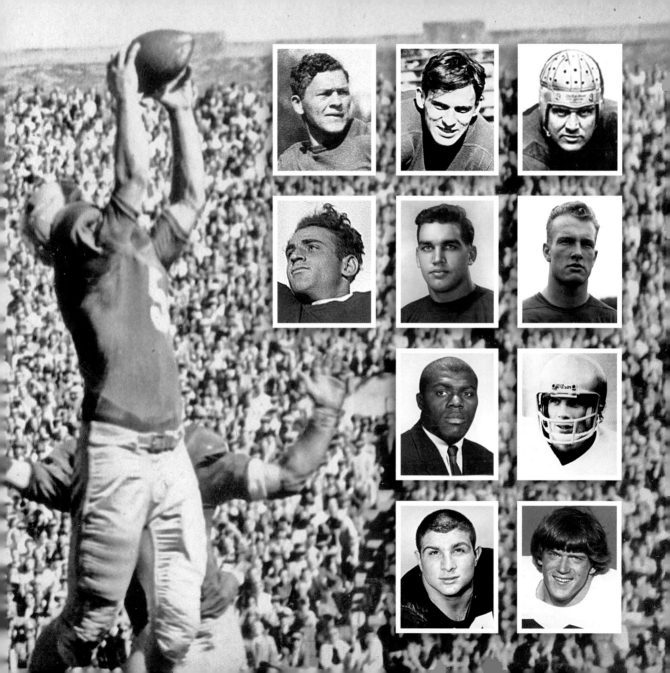

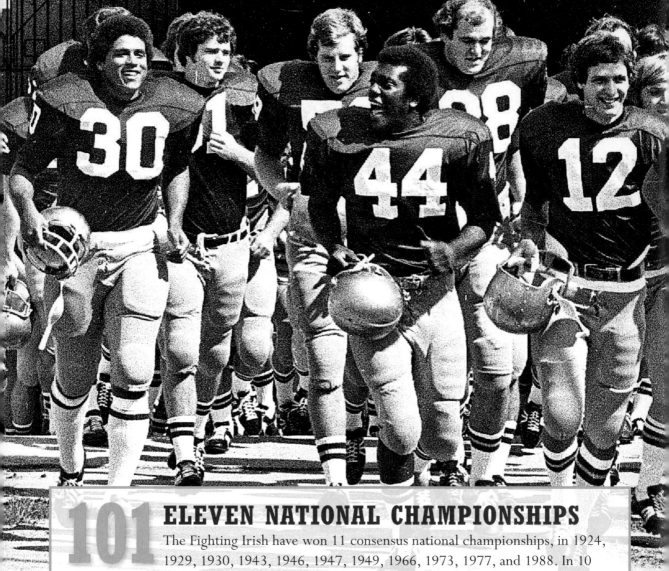

101 ELEVEN NATIONAL CHAMPIONSHIPS

The Fighting Irish have won 11 consensus national championships, in 1924, 1929, 1930, 1943, 1946, 1947, 1949, 1966, 1973, 1977, and 1988. In 10 other years, Notre Dame has been recognized as the national champion by one or more organizations. No other program has more.

Ara Parseghian leads his team onto the field, 1973.

The Four Horsemen, left to right: Don Miller, Harry Stuhldreher, Jim Crowley, and Elmer Layden

ACKNOWLEDGMENTS

This book has been a real pleasure to write and produce. Football at Notre Dame, so rich in history and tradition, offers hundreds, if not thousands, of reasons to love it, and culling it down to just 101 was one of the most difficult tasks I faced.

So many people had a part in preparing this book for publication:

First and foremost, a special word of thanks goes out to Ann Stratton, Leslie Stoker, and all the good people at Stewart, Tabori & Chang. It's a real pleasure to work with folks who believe in the beauty, joy, and power of books.

And to Richard Slovak, our brilliant copy editor, who makes sure every little detail is correct, it's great having him on the team.

I would also like to thank my dear friends Mary Tiegreen and Hubert Pedroli, who do so much to help the process along, as well as serving as a second family to me.

Thanks to Bob Griffin, a Notre Dame graduate, and his family, for their continuing friendship and generous spirit.

To Ted Ciuzio and his associates at AP Images, and Tim Williams and his staff and Collegiate Images, thank you for all your time and effort. And to Bob Nelson, who supplied the program from the 1966 Notre Dame–Michigan State game, your generosity is greatly appreciated.

To my family, Mary, Savannah, Dakota, and Sam; my parents, Ron and Beth; brother Ron and sister Edie; and the rest of the Greens, McGlones, and Mathwichs, I couldn't have done it without you. Thanks a million.

And to everyone at Notre Dame: players coaches, administrators, teachers, students, and fans— you make it all so special. Rah, rah, for Notre Dame!

 **A Tiegreen Book**

Published in 2009 by Stewart, Tabori & Chang
An imprint of ABRAMS

Text copyright © 2009 David Green
Compilation copyright © 2009 Mary Tiegreen

All rights reserved. No portion of this book may be repro-
duced, stored in a retrieval system, or transmitted in any
form or by any means, mechanical, electronic, photocopying,
recording, or otherwise, without written permission from the
publisher.

Editor: Ann Stratton
Designer: David Green, Brightgreen Design
Production Manager: Tina Cameron

Stewart, Tabori & Chang books are available at special dis-
counts when purchased in quantity for premiums and promo-
tions as well as fundraising or educational use. Special editions
can also be created to specification. For details, contact
specialmarkets@hnabooks.com.

101 Reasons to Love Notre Dame Football is a book in the
101 REASONS TO LOVE™ series.

101 REASONS TO LOVE™ is a trademark of
Mary Tiegreen and Hubert Pedroli.

Library of Congress Cataloging-in-Publication Data

Green, David.
  101 reasons to love Notre Dame Football / David Green.
    p. cm. -- (101 reasons to love)
  Includes bibliographical references and index.
  ISBN 978-1-58479-811-8 (alk. paper)
  1. Notre Dame Fighting Irish (Football team)--History. 2.
University of
Notre Dame--Football--History. I. Title. II. Title: One hundred
one reasons
to love Notre Dame Football. III. Title: One hundred and one
reasons to love
Notre Dame Football.
  GV958.N6G74 2009
  796.332'630977289--dc22

                          2009012576

Printed and bound in China
10 9 8 7 6 5 4 3 2 1

THE ART OF BOOKS SINCE 1949

115 West 18th Street
New York, NY 10011
www.abramsbooks.com

Photo Credits

AP Images: pages 1, 2–3, 10, 16 (inset), 18–19, 20, 21, 24 (inset), 28–29, 30–31, 36, 39, 40–41, 43, 44 (inset), 47, 50, 51 (inset), 52–53, 54–55, 56 (inset), 57, 58 (inset), 60, 61, 62 (inset), 62–63, 65, 67 (portrait), 68–69, 71 (inset), 75, 78, 80, 81, 84 (inset), 85, 88, 89, 91, 95, 98 (ball), 99, 101, 102 (inset), 102–103, 104, 106, 108–109, 112, 113 (inset), 115 (Lambeau, McNally, and Montana insets), 116–117

Notre Dame/Collegiate Images: pages 4–5, 6–7, 9, 11 (inset), 13, 14, 15 (inset), 16–17, 22–23, 24–25, 26, 32, 35, 45, 46, 48, 52, 59, 67, 70–71, 76, 82, 86 (inset), 87, 92, 96 (inset), 97, 107, 111, 114–115, 115 (Millner, Connor, Hornung, Page, Buoniconti, and Casper insets), 118

David Green: pages 33 (pennant), 38 (card), 90 (card), 110 (program), 115 (Trafton inset)

Bob Nelson: page 63 (program)

Getty Images/TimeLifePictures.com: page 72